ON DUCATI

1982-1991

Reprinted From
Cycle World Magazine

ISBN 1 85520 2069

Published By
Brooklands Books with permission of Cycle World

We are frequently asked for copies of out of print Road Tests and other articles that have appeared in Cycle World. To satisfy this need we are producing a series of books that will include, as nearly as possible, all the important information on one make or subject for a given period.

It is our hope that these collections of articles will give an overview that will be of value to historians, restorers and potential buyers, as well as to present owners of these interesting motorcycles.

CYCLE WORLD

Italy's Newest V-Twin is Dedicated to Sport, Pure and Simple

■ There are times when riding a Ducati Pantah is magic, as when hurtling along a gently-curved, deserted highway, surrounded by fields of green spring grass, enveloped in a rush of warm air, the speedometer needle bent over hard right and the beat of the exhaust lost behind in the speed.

And there are times when riding a Ducati Pantah is a chore, as when bucking along a sagging section of concrete freeway in heavy traffic, kidneys crying for support, wrists aching and locked at an odd angle, the engine stumbling and hesitating with each tiny movement of the twist grip.

There may be motorcycles that can't make up their mind what they're supposed to be or do, but the Pantah is not among them. The Pantah is a sport bike, built to run hard and fast and not to languish in the crush of urban congestion.

Its purpose is obvious from the first glance—the styling carries road racer looks beyond hints and suggestions into the Grand Prix world of fairings and clip-on handlebars and streamlined tailsections.

The Pantah carries Ducati's latest engine, the most recent in a line of 90° V-Twins dating back to the late 1960s when the company lashed together two 250cc Singles to build a 500cc racebike. The original engine was enlarged and refined into a 750, the basis for the current 900s (which are actually 860cc). Throughout the evolution, the Ducati Vees sold to the public retained 40° (from vertical) valve angle, two valves per cylinder, roller-bearing crankshaft and sohc with each cam driven by a shaft and four bevel gears.

Ever-tightening government regulations—both in Europe and America—on allowable sound levels, the performance lessons learned in 13 years of racing the older Vees, and the high cost of producing the 900 engine all were major considerations in the design of the Pantah engine.

The new engine started with 498.9cc in the Pantah 500, with bore and stroke of 74 x 58mm. It was enlarged to the 583cc Pantah 600 by increasing bore to 80mm. It's still a 90° air-cooled V-Twin with sohc, two valves per cylinder and desmo valve gear (more on this later). But the Pantah has a plain bearing crankshaft and its camshafts are driven by toothed rubber belts, four sprockets and two belts replacing the shafts and gears used in the older engine. The belts are quieter and cheaper and have proven reliable in automotive (and Honda Gold Wing) applications.

Beyond the change in the type of camshaft drive, the desire to reduce noise shows up in the form of rubber pads partially surrounding the cam drive belt sprockets and in the placement of 60 individual rattle-damping rubber bushings between cylinder cooling fins.

The switch from the roller-bearing crankshaft of the 900s to the Pantah's plain-bearing crankshaft made sense in several ways. The 900's built-up roller bearing crankshafts were expensive to build, contributed to mechanical noise, and had a racing life measured in hours. The Pantah's plain-bearing crank with two-piece rods and insert bearings is less expensive to make, runs quieter and has improved racing durability. It's also lighter.

The Pantah crankshaft, like the crank used in the 900 engine, has a single throw carrying the two connecting rods side-by-›

side. The rod for the front cylinder is to the right of the rod for the rear cylinder, so the front cylinder is offset to the right.

The Ducati's 90° Vee is wider than most, gaining several advantages. A 90° V-Twin offers perfect primary balance, and allows plenty of room for the placement of carburetors and exhausts to best performance advantage. It's also easier to cool the rear cylinder of a wider Vee. A disadvantage is that a 90° V-Twin is expensive to produce because the almost-horizontal front cylinder and head must be different castings than the rear cylinder to ensure that cooling fins match the direction of airflow. Another disadvantage is that—all other things being equal—wider V-Twin engines require a longer wheelbase than narrower Vees, again because the front cylinder is almost horizontal.

Like all V-Twins, the Ducati's firing order is staggered. If it were a parallel Twin, one cylinder would fire, and 360° of crankshaft rotation later, the second cylinder would fire. But because the cylinders are arranged 90° apart, the rear cylinder fires 270° (360° minus 90°) after the front cylinder, and the front cylinder fires again 450° (360° plus 90°) after the rear cylinder.

Experience gained in 13 years of campaigning the older Vees figures heavily in the design of the Pantah's cylinder heads. The 900s were limited by intake port and combustion chamber shape, both related to the 900's valve angle of 40° from vertical.

The Pantah, like the factory's successful short-stroke racing 750 of the early '70s, has a 30° valve angle and ports that drop into the combustion chambers. The valve angle allows a more compact combustion chamber and a lower piston dome for the 9.5:1 c.r., and the lower piston dome combines with the port shape to improve breathing.

The intake valves measure 37.5mm, the exhaust valves 33.5mm. The camshafts open the intake valves 50° BTDC and close them 80° ABDC; the exhaust valves open 75° BBDC and close 45° ATDC.

Ducatis have been sold with conventional valve springs and with desmodromic (desmo for short) valve gear, in which one rocker arm opens a valve, and a second rocker arm pulls it shut, each rocker arm activated by its own cam lobe, one cam lobe mirroring the other so as one arm rises the other falls and vice versa.

Desmo engines have become the unofficial trademark of Ducati, and the system was developed for racing long ago when poor valve spring quality led to problems with valve float and spring breakage. Because the valves in a desmo

er—the shims listed in the parts book don't come in small enough increments to allow precise valve clearances. Fortunately, once broken in, many desmo Ducatis maintain correct opening and closing clearances over long periods of time, in some cases 10,000 mi. and beyond.

The rubber cam belts are driven off the right end of a shaft located between the cylinders. The other end of that shaft is gear driven off the left end of the crankshaft. The cams run in ball bearings pressed into the head castings.

The pistons used in the Pantah are forged and carry three rings, two compression and a one-piece oil control. The cylinders are aluminum without iron liners. Instead of using the usual pressed-in liners, the cylinder bores are chemically coated with a combination of nickel and a small percentage of ceramic silicon carbide particles. The nickel in the mixture holds the silicon carbide particles in place, and the particles themselves, which are only slightly less hard than diamonds, act as the wear surface. Because silicon carbide resists galling, the surface is less prone to seizure than either a chrome-plated bore or an iron bore. The surface is very durable, but if it is damaged, the entire cylinder must be replaced.

Primary drive is via helical gear and the conventional multi-plate clutch is operated hydraulically. The transmission has five speeds and the final drive sprocket is mounted directly on the countershaft. The drive chain is 530 non-O-ring Diamond chain.

Each cylinder is fed by its own 36mm Dell'Orto with accelerator pump, and each carb draws air through a long rubber elbow running up to a single cylindrical airbox and pleated paper element. The ignition is inductive electronic using a Bosch control box and Nippondenso coils. Ignition advance is electronically controlled. There is an electric starter and no provision for kick start.

The Pantah has dual exhausts joined underneath the engine by a crossover tube/expansion box designed to increase mid-range power. Huge Conti mufflers eliminate most of the throaty V-Twin staggered exhaust beat.

The Ducati's frame is built up of small tubes, the main structure formed like a bridge truss instead of the more common motorcycle frame using a single large backbone tube or a pair of tubes. The design originated in racing and is very rigid without being heavy. There is no engine cradle and no tubes run underneath the motor. The engine hangs below the frame, (a design also used by Yamaha) and is a stressed member. Two engine mount bolts are located between the cylinders, two behind the rear

cylinder, and two more at the bottom rear of the crankcases, matching a set of rear section tubes extending from the main frame. The rear section tubes also carry upper mounts for the gas-charged Marzocchi shock absorbers.

The swing arm pivot shaft runs through the rear of the engine cases and is supported by two plain bushings located inside the cases and lubricated by engine oil. The steering head stem rides in tapered roller bearings.

Steering head rake is 30.5°, and wheelbase is 57 in. Wheels are cast magnesium, a WM3-18 front and a WM4-18 rear, and come mounted with a Michelin S41 front tire and a Michelin M45 rear tire.

The Pantah's half fairing is made of fiberglass in two sections, bolted together across a central seam, with a plexiglass bubble windscreen. The fairing is mounted to the frame with a pylon mount running from the steering head (between the fork tubes) and a side mount bolted to the frame just above the front cylinder head. The front fairing mount also carries the quartz 55/60w headlight, the choke lever and the cable-driven Nippondenso speedometer and tachometer. A row of lights is positioned between the instruments, indicating lights and high beam turn signal use, neutral selection, loss of oil pressure, alternator failure, or sidestand deployment (although there isn't a sidestand). The front turn signals are rectangular and built into the fairing on each side. The rear turn signals are round and mount on stalks from the rear fender.

Clip-on handlebars are positioned just below the upper triple clamp and carry Japanese electrical switches and Brembo master cylinders, one for the front brakes and one for the hydraulic clutch.

The combination of the half fairing and the clip-on handlebars seriously restricts the Pantah's steering lock, which means driveway and parking lot maneuvering is clumsy, requiring back-and-forth Y-turns.

The Pantah carries three 10.25-in., drilled-cast-iron Brembo discs, two in the front and one in the rear. Twin Brembo calipers mount to the center-axle front forks, which have 35mm stanchion tubes, and a single Brembo caliper mounts beneath the swing arm.

The fenders, side panels, rear section and seat base are fiberglass; the gas tank is steel. The seat is secured by three bolts, one on each side and one at the rear. A fiberglass cover can be bolted in place to hide the rear section of the seat or removed to allow room for a passenger or soft luggage. The side panels are each held by two short prongs, which fit into rubber grommets on the frame, and a

engine are mechanically closed instead of relying on spring pressure, valve float is impossible. In the desmo Pantah engine, there is a small, hairpin spring attached to each valve to positively seat the valve for starting, but that spring is of no consequence after start up.

The valve-closing rocker arm is forked and fits underneath a top-hat-shaped collar positioned below retainer clips on the valve stem. A winkler cap shim fits on top of the end of the valve stem, and the opening rocker arm pushes against the winkler cap. Clearances must be set for both rocker assemblies, and those clearances are adjusted by winkler caps and collars of different thicknesses.

It's a clever system, but adjustment requires a fair amount of disassembly, including the removal of rocker arm shafts. The most time-consuming part of the job, experienced Ducati mechanics tell us, is sizing the shims on a surface grind-

DUCATI 600SL PANTAH

Nippondenso instruments on the Pantah aren't accurate and the odometer reads in kilometers. Ignition switch hides underneath a rubber cap.

Brembo front brake system works flawlessly, in spite of uncomfortable lever. Tire is a Michelin S41. Handlebars clip to fork tubes.

The Ducati's frame is built up of small tubes and the engine hangs below. Electrics are a mix of Italian, German and Japanese. Note oil level sight glass in the sidecase.

Part of the fiberglass tail section can be removed to reveal a passenger seat.

single bolt. Those bolts screw into ordinary 8mm nuts cast into the fiberglass tailsection, and it's too easy to dislodge the nuts when replacing the side panels.

For all its sports styling, the Pantah is not especially fast. At the dragstrip, the Pantah logged a best elapsed time of 13.95 sec. with a terminal speed of 94.24 mph. Top speed in the half mile was 108 mph. That's slightly faster than the BMW R65LS, which turned 13.99 sec. and 93.16 mph in the quarter and reached 101 mph in the half mile, but slower than the 552cc Yamaha V-Twin Vision, which ran 13.09 sec. at 96.87 mph in the quarter. The 550 Fours are even quicker; the Yamaha Seca turned 13.06 sec. and 97.82 mph, the Kawasaki GPz550 did 12.70 sec. and 102.04 mph. In the half mile, the Vision reached 110 mph, the Seca 111 mph and the GPz 116 mph.

Part of the reason lies with the way the Pantah is geared. Our test bike, which we rented from Champion Motorcycles in Costa Mesa, California, was delivered with a 15-tooth countershaft sprocket and a 36-tooth rear sprocket. With that gearing, the Pantah could theoretically reach 138 mph at its 9050 rpm redline in fifth gear, or 116 mph at redline in fourth gear. In actual fact, there's no way the Pantah will pull the tall gearing in fourth, let alone fifth.

Because the Pantah is geared so tall, it is difficult to leave a stop quickly, and several downshifts are required for quickly passing traffic on the highway.

With stock gearing, the Pantah turns 3935 rpm at 60 mph. That's a lot less than the average 550: the Vision turns 5295 rpm at 60, the Seca 4932 rpm and the GPz 4625 rpm.

However, there is no way a Pantah pilot could discern the actual relationship between rpm and road speed, because both of the Nippondenso instruments are wildly optimistic. The tachometer on our test bike read 1000 rpm higher than actual engine speed, and the speedometer showed 60 mph at an actual 54 mph. So, from the rider's seat, the bike seems to be traveling almost 70 mph and turning about 5000 rpm at an actual 60 mph and 3935 rpm.

To see what effect more realistic gearing would have, we installed a 40-tooth rear sprocket and returned to the dragstrip. The Pantah instantly went half a second quicker, with the best run stopping the clocks at 13.40 sec. and 97.61 mph. Regeared, the Pantah was easy to launch. Instead of bogging off the line, it often spun the rear tire. Pre-start burnouts increased tire traction and led to the quickest elapsed times.

With the lower gearing, the Pantah turned 4379 rpm at an actual 60 mph, and maximum theoretical speed in fifth dropped to 124 mph, a figure still beyond reach. Maximum speed in fourth dropped to an attainable 104 mph.

Top speed in the half mile stayed at 108 mph despite the gearing change, bringing us to the second reason the Pantah is not as quick as other 550s—it doesn't make as much horsepower.

Nor is it much lighter, weighing 432 lb. with half a tank of gas, compared to the Vision's 462 lb., the GPz's 459 lb. and the Seca's 424 lb. It does feel lighter,

Pantah's overhead camshafts are driven by toothed rubber belts off a shaft running between the cylinders. Each cylinder has its own 36mm Dell'Orto carburetor, with accelerator pump.

Twin cylinders are at 90° angle. Sight glass in lefthand case is for viewing timing marks with a strobe light. A spin-on oil filter fits into the bottom of the vertically-split crankcases.

because the forward cylinder is almost horizontal, significantly lowering the center of gravity.

Which is a good thing, because with a 57-in. wheelbase, 30.5° of rake and clip-on handlebars, it's already slower steering than any of the Japanese 550s. While all the Japanese models have about the same wheelbase, all also have steeper rake angles (averaging 27°) and wider handlebars, making them more willing to change direction quickly. The Ducati, however, if not having an actual advantage, comes back into the thick of things in S-turns, where the lower center of gravity makes it easier to lift the bike up from a turn in one direction and throw it into a turn in the other direction.

And the Ducati is dead stable under all conditions, unperturbed by fast sweeping turns or bumps or anything else, which, of course, is what the Italians had in mind when designing the chassis and selecting rake and wheelbase.

The Pantah could have steered quicker with less rake angle and a shorter wheelbase, but stability was chosen over maximum agility. The Pantah does have excellent cornering clearance with tires to match. There is no sidestand, and the first thing to drag on the left side is the centerstand lift tang. Dragging that takes serious lean, and scraping the rearset footpegs while the motorcycle is still on its wheels is impossible. On the right, the exhaust system scrapes first. Cornering clearance is not a problem.

The Pantah has no peer in braking power and control. The Brembo levers themselves are substandard when compared to the levers used on Japanese bikes, being located too far from the handlebar grips and having a square-edged shape which doesn't conform well to the human hand. A set of dogleg levers would make it easier for normal-sized riders to use the brakes (and clutch). But once past that annoyance, a light pull on the lever produces considerable braking force, and the front wheel can be locked. The excellence comes in how easily the front wheel can be held on the edge of tire-squalling lockup, and in how predictable the brakes are when leaning into a corner. The Pantah's stopping ability is due to an intelligent choice of leverage ratios and system stiffness. Once the lever is pulled to the point where the pads are against the discs, the lever stops moving. From then on, pressure is the controlling factor. Pull the lever harder and the result is more braking force at the tire, all in a wonderfully linear fashion.

The rear brake requires more pressure for a given amount of braking power than the rear brakes on most other motorcycles. Consequently it can be used hard without fear of locking when heavy front-wheel braking is unloading the rear wheel.

The Pantah stopped from 60 mph in 120 ft., and from 30 mph in 33.5 ft. The stopping distance from 60 mph is noteworthy when compared to the 134, 133 and 128 ft. required by the GPz, Vision and Seca, respectively.

A Pantah pilot will feel more vibration in the handlebars and footpegs than a rider on a rubber-mounted Four, but what vibration the Pantah produces isn't excessive. At some engine speeds the Pantah is smooth enough that the rear-view mirrors (not included in the base price) are crystal clear. At other engine speeds the bars buzz.

Which, combined with the fact that the rider must support his upper torso weight at any legal speed, can cause hands to become numb during a prolonged ride.

The riding position, so well-suited for jaunts at more than 100 mph, is a major fatigue factor at slower speeds. So, too, is the suspension system, which works well enough at very high speeds but which pounds the rider incessantly at more common speeds, especially over uneven road surfaces or concrete highways. The hard seat could double as a church pew in Puritanical Boston, or maybe as a sawhorse.

The carburetion is flawed as well, with a stumble and hesitation when the throttle is opened at an indicated 5000 rpm, regardless of road speed or other conditions. The condition is most pronounced when the throttle is opened after being held steady at or near 5000 rpm and is caused by excessive leanness at that point. Raising the slide needle one notch helped, but did not eliminate the problem, and we can only wonder how bad it would be if the Pantah did not have accelerator pumps.

At other throttle openings, the Pantah runs rich, briefly belching black puffs of smoke when the throttle is briskly opened and coating the exhaust system insides with soot. The carburetion is rich enough that the chokes don't have to be used for cold starts, excepting freezing mornings.

Riding the Pantah requires three keys—one for the ignition switch, which is located on the instrument panel, one for the locking gas cap, and one for the fork lock built into the side of the steering head.

The Ducati's paint and decals are substandard to the least expensive Japanese motorcycles. The horn isn't much better, emitting a weak squawk instead of the strident warning we've come to expect of sporting Italian machines. And the turn signals don't blink so much as stutter rapidly.

The Ducati Pantah is a very expensive motorcycle, selling for about $5000, and it requires an unusual amount of understanding and patience from its owner. The idea of rider comfort hasn't come of age at the Ducati factory, and there isn't much of a distribution system for the bikes in the U.S. The few dealers who do sell Ducatis don't as a rule stock many parts, and while the owner of a Japanese motorcycle stands a fair chance of buying, say, clutch plates off the shelf, a Ducati owner must wait until the parts are ordered and delivered.

What the Ducati has going for it is its differentness, its birthplace, its acceptance as an object of interest.

The Pantah is fun to ride, rewarding in its own specialized way. But we suspect the only people who will buy one are people whom for whatever reason, really, really want a Pantah. ◨

DUCATI 600SL PANTAH

SPECIFICATIONS

List price $4949
Engine ...... sohc V-Twin
Bore x stroke .. 80 x 58mm
Displacement 583cc
Compression ratio ... 9.5:1
Carburetion .....(2) 36mm
Dell'Orto
Air filter ..... pleated paper
Ignition . inductive electronic
Claimed power .. 58 bhp @
8500 rpm
Claimed torque . 37 lb.-ft. @
7500 rpm
Lubrication ..... wet sump
Oil capacity .... 3 qt.
Fuel capacity ..... 4.8 gal.
Starter .... electric
Electrical power 200w
alternator
Battery 12v 14ah
Headlight 55/60w
Primary drive .. helical gear
Clutch .... multi-plate, wet
Final drive ...... 530 chain
Gear ratios, overall: 1
5th 4.81
4th 5.74
3rd 7.12
2nd 9.16
1st 13.35
Suspension:
Front .... telescopic forks
travel .... 5 in.
Rear .... swing arm
travel .... 3.5 in.
Tires:
Front 3.25-in. H-18
Michelin S41
Rear 3.50 H-18
Michelin M45
Brakes
Front .. dual 10.25-in. disc
Rear .... 10.25-in. disc
Brake swept area 247 sq. in.
Brake loading (160lb.
rider) ..... 2.40 lb./sq. in.
Wheelbase .... 57 in.
Rake/Trail .... 30.5°/5.1 in.
Handlebar width .... 24 in.
Seat height .... 31 in.
Seat width .... 7 in.
Footpeg height .... 14.5 in.
Ground clearance ..... 6 in.
Test weight (w/half-tank
fuel .... 432 lb.
Weight bias,
% front/rear 45/55
GVWR .... 871 lb.
Load capacity ..... 439 lb.

ACCELERATION

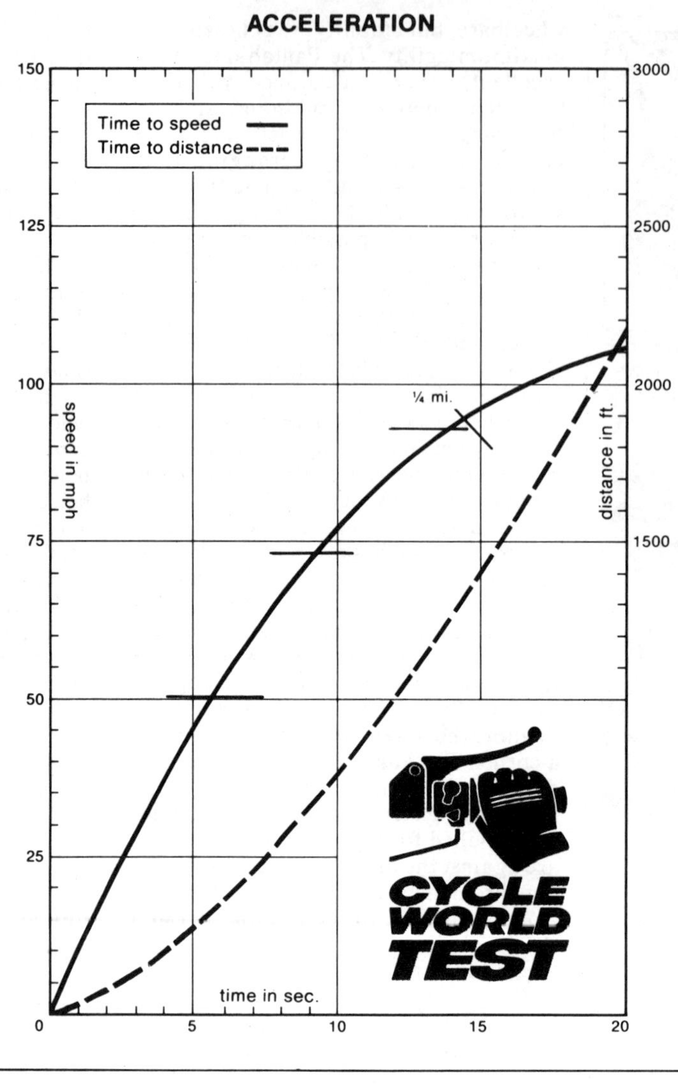

PERFORMANCE

Standing ¼-mile . 13.95 sec.
@ 94.24 mph
Top speed in ½-mile 108 mph
Fuel consumption .. 50 mpg
Range
(to reserve tank) . 211 mi.
Acceleration:
0–30 mph ..... 2.4 sec.
0–40 mph ..... 3.6 sec.
0–50 mph ..... 4.8 sec.
0–60 mph ..... 6.5 sec.
0–70 mph ..... 7.7 sec.
0–80 mph .... 10.3 sec.
0–90 mph .... 13.1 sec.
0–100 mph .... 16.2 sec.
Top gear acceleration:
40–60 mph .... 10.3 sec.
60–80 mph ..... 8.7 sec.
Maximum speeds in gears
@ 9050 rpm:
1st .... 50 mph
2nd .... 73 mph
3rd .... 93 mph
4th .... 116 mph
5th .... 138 mph
Speedometer error:
30 mph indicated 26 mph
60 mph indicated 54 mph
Braking distance:
from 30 mph ...... 33 ft.
from 60 mph ..... 120 ft.
Engine speed
at 60 mph .... 3935 rpm

LA CARRERA

The Ducati Montjuich was the perfect bike for La Carrera— fast, light and stable.

PHOTOS BY DAVID EDWARDS

RON "GOMEZ" GRIEWE, CYCLE WORLD'S SENIOR editor, a grizzled pre-runner and non-finisher of a half-dozen Baja races, was expounding.

"You might as well carry some plastic flowers with you, and a white cross. Then, when a Mexican rancher in a pickup truck runs you off the road at 120, you'll have a chance to stick them in the ground as you go flying past. It'll save the organizers the trouble." Ron's inimitable barking laughter capped his advice.

I smiled, but Griewe's humor seemed all too pointed. What had I done in entering La Carrera Costa a Costa? A race from Ensenada, on the Pacific coast of the Baja peninsula, to San Felipe, a sleepy resort 140 miles east on the Sea of Cortez, La Carrera was to cover the entire distance on Mexican highways. The American organizers of the race, Loyal Truesdale and ex-Kawasaki-racer Cliff Carr, insisted that the Mexican Federales would have the road thoroughly closed. But anyone who knew Baja, and the myriad of small dirt roads and trails branching from that main highway, found that claim difficult to believe.

Not only that, I had escalated the stakes. La Carrera rules limited eligible motorcycles to Singles and Twins in an effort to keep speeds within reason, and I had originally thought of entering a dual-purpose Single. The slightly over-100-mph top speed of a Single seemed a good match for the bumpy, narrow, shoulderless two-lane that twisted its way out of Ensenada. But a real racebike—a Cagiva-Ducati Montjuich—had fallen into *Cycle World*'s hands, and I couldn't resist using it. Maybe it was *too* fast; I'd just be careful.

Still, the week before the race was a nervous time; I was concerned about my safety, and my ego. My not-entirely successful club-racing career ended six years ago, and I had no illusions about being the world's fastest street rider. And every phone call to the organizers brought tales of a quicker-yet entrant. A Ducati dealer from Santa Barbara was bringing a 1000cc Ducati engine housed in a Harris frame; there was a Moto Guzzi Battle-of-the-Twins bike coming from Arizona; Isle of Man winner Dave Roper was contesting the Vintage class with his ageless, and very fast, Matchless G50. Rough competition all, and rougher yet in pre-race imagination as pictures of 150-mph BMWs and Guzzis and Ducatis danced in my head.

When I finally arrived at race headquarters at the Bahia Hotel in Ensenada, the parking lot was full of competitors, but few who lived up to those images. There was a contingent of Ducati-philes from Santa Barbara with an awning stretched between their vans, and banners hung, forming a professional-looking pit that housed the trick 1000cc Ducati. But its frame was a Harris replica that wasn't completely successful, and its owner had elected to ride a better-handling Cagiva Alazzurra instead. There were plenty of big Ducatis around, but none was Battle-of-the Twins serious. In equal abundance were modified dual-purpose machines on trailers behind station wagons, including some Kawasaki-supplied KLR600s. They were to carry former national champions Gary Nixon and Mark Brelsford, who had been lured down to Baja by old racing compatriot Cliff Carr. Nixon "just wanted to see what it was all about," while Brelsford had a more specific interest: "I'm sick of the 55-mph limit, and want a chance to run flat-out without worrying about cops." Dick Mann brought the number of former national champions to three, but he had arrived at the last minute, without a bike. Unless something could be scrounged,

BY STEVE ANDERSON

11

Dodging goats and pickups at 140 mph: Roadracing, Mexican-style.

Mufflers may be required, but you'd never know it from the booming and bellowing of the four-stroke Singles and Twins entered in the race.

A wide variety of machines were entered, from classic Nortons to slightly more modern ones, from Triumph Twins to Honda CX500s. Most Exotic award may go to Honda XR600 engine in a 500 Interceptor frame.

he'd merely pit for Brelsford and Nixon.

Pre-running on Friday morning before Saturday's race demonstrated that the course was challenging. The first 30 miles passed through low mountains, with 50- to 100-mph turns merging together, or connected by only the shortest of straights. The road surface was macadam, with loose gravel at the edges, and bumps and tar strips in corners where cars had scrubbed away gravel. Run-off was non-existent; most corners were cut into a cliff on one side, with a sheer drop on the other.

After that, the course opened up, with miles-long straights ending in high-speed sweeping turns that led to more straights. Can you say "fast"? Seventy miles out from Ensenada the pace slowed through the tight turns of the pass that drops into Valle de Trinidad. This small town marked the halfway point, time to stop for gas. From there on was desert road, a straight ribbon laid over undulating terrain, a high-speed roller-coaster ride broken only by a few broad turns, and a brief tight section through the echoes of a rocky canyon. Finally, a sweeping turn dumped onto *the* straight, 30 miles of road laid out with God's own straightedge, a final engine durability test before San Felipe.

This initial look at the course left me with doubts about my own willingness to attack such an unforgiving road, but a check later that afternoon of the Montjuich's gearing offered some encouragement. On a long straight, the little red-and-silver Duck showed 9400 rpm in top gear, well over 140 mph—just what La Carrera demanded. The race looked interesting yet.

As the start approached on Saturday morning, the competition was becoming clearer. David Roper, on the old Matchless Single, seemed the *rider* to beat, but was likely to be held back by his under-130-mph top speed. Some of the big Dukes would be fast, but probably not faster than the Montjuich, and certainly not as nimble. Most threatening of all was Rick Mitchell, who was riding a standard Ducati F1. An employee of *Motorcycle Industry Magazine* and a regular club racer, Rick had just participated in Honda's 24-hour world-record attempt, where he had actually enjoyed going 160 mph during the night sessions. That alone qualified him as a potential La Carrera winner, but he had failed to re-gear his F1. That reassured me; if I could only stay close to him through the early twisties, the Montjuich would restore on the straights any time I might lose in the corners.

Then it was time to race. A rag-tag parade through Ensenada degenerated into noisy lane-splitting, with the 35 motorcycle entrants weaving in and out between round-shouldered pickup trucks and smoking cars before we finally arrived at the starting line six miles from the city. Proving that La Carrera was indeed a Mexican race, the start was delayed, and as we sat cooking on our bikes in the hot sun, the Mexican police were also proving the Baja veterans right by waving cars past us onto the course. Loyal Truesdale used the delay to determine the starting order; the fastest bikes would go first, two at a time, each pair one minute apart. The race results would be calculated on overall time.

Mitchell and I, on the two Ducati F1s, were first off the line. He led, and I tucked in behind. Rick was riding harder than I wanted, so I concentrated on being smooth and keeping him in sight. But the adrenaline of my first race in years was propelling me quicker than I had ever expected to run, and as rock walls and vistas rushed past, I was only slowly losing ground. By the time we finished

Tecate beer was a sponsor of La Carrera, and provided cold cerveza for everyone at the finish. From the right: Rick Mitchell, 2nd place overall; Nick Ienatsch, 5th overall and 1st 650; and the author.

Gary Nixon was among the former national champions in attendance; he liked the race, but thought his KLR600 could have used more speed on the straightaways.

Dick Mann, who has more than a slight familiarity with the Matchless G50, confers with David Roper on a plug reading.

with the tight corners, I was down only 30 or 40 seconds; soon, the long straights allowed the Montjuich to reel in Mitchell, putting me into the lead. A perfect gas stop, executed by *Cycle World* shop foreman Dave Pedersen, enlarged that lead, and I was left with enjoying the ride and trying not to do anything stupid.

The rest of the ride was hardly boring. Small, dark shapes far down the road on one straight resolved themselves into a herd of goats, forcing a drop to a near walking pace before the bellow of the Montjuich chased them away. And the vados—long dips where economical Mexican highway engineers dropped the road to sandwash level instead of building a bridge that would be required only during the rainy season—were equally interesting. On one of the more abrupt drops, at over 140 mph, the Montjuich suddenly went light, and the engine's song shot up an octave; I was still in a tuck when we landed 100 feet farther down the road, softly, fortunately, and with the front wheel straight. I can honestly say there was no fear; there wasn't time. I did, however, roll the throttle back for later vados.

More danger was presented by cars and trucks on the course; closing speeds for the vehicles we were passing approached 80 mph, and 200 mph for the oncoming traffic. Fortunately, there were no accidents, even if David Roper did come close; he rounded a corner to find not one but *two* pickup trucks taking up the road. He squeaked by on the far right edge before the passing truck could move back over.

My Montjuich crossed the finish line first, having taken 1 hour, 17 minutes and 4 seconds to cover 140.4 miles, a 109-mph average. Mitchell came across two minutes later, for second place. Later, after the times were tabulated, David Roper finished third overall, both first vintage and first 500, with a 1:20:27; Fred Eiker, a regular Battle-of-the-Twins competitor, managed a fourth, ahead of all the big Ducatis, in 1:21:21 on a Norton 850. Eiker may have put in the ride of the race; his Norton had run out of gas once, forcing him to coast into his gas stop.

But for most of the entrants, this race wasn't about winning. It was about blasting down roads as fast as you cared to go, without worrying about the police. It was about the bench-racing in the pits and after the race, and the chance to hear about Mark Brelsford's eventful pit stop, where he was doused with a crotchful of gasoline. (This planned pit stop led to a second, impromptu, stop to allow Brelsford to dispose of his gasoline-logged underwear. Other La Carrera competitors reported seeing a strange, naked man dancing in obvious pain by the roadside). It was about the party afterward in San Felipe.

But for me, La Carrera was a Ducati Montjuich singing sharply at over 9000 rpm, a song so sweet I hated to roll off the throttle for the turns. It was flying over vados at 140, and zipping past cars at twice or three times their speed. And it sure didn't hurt to win. ◙

CAGIVA-DUCATI F1 MONTJUICH

RAUCOUS, RED, AND 11 SECONDS FAST

PHOTO BY STAN SHOLIK

CYCLE WORLD

PHOTO BY RICH CHENET

DUCATI
Montjuich
DUCATI
MARVIC

SOMEWHERE, SOMEPLACE, THERE MUST BE A MAN who has heard only Muzak. Surrounded by its innocuous melodies in elevators and department stores, he may have finding it vaguely pleasant, and thought it as involving as music could be.

Imagine, then, this sheltered man found himself at a Rolling Stones concert. Sitting in a darkened concert hall, he'd be caught by the crowd's hush and anticipation before the start. His heart would begin beating faster. Then a wall of light and sound would overtake him, beat itself upon him. And like it or not, he'd be a million miles from Muzak.

Somewhere, someplace, there also must be people who believe that today's popular sportbikes represent the pinnacle of the motorcycling experience. A single ride on a Ducati Montjuich would shatter that belief as thoroughly as a Stones concert questions Muzak.

As red as a Ferrari, its filterless velocity stacks all agleam, the Montjuich makes no pretense of subtlety. Even its 1500-rpm idle is as lumpy and nasty as that of a race-cammed, open-piped V-Eight. Click down into first gear and accelerate hard, and the bike lifts its front wheel like a 747 on take-off, but with the thunder of a NASCAR stocker instead of the whoosh of a jet.

This is a Twin that will cover a quarter-mile in the high elevens, with only a grabby clutch and a short wheelbase preventing it from running a few tenths quicker. This is a Twin that will run with, or even pull slightly, a Suzuki GSX-R750 down the long front straight at Willow Springs. In short, this is the quickest production Twin *Cycle World* has ever tested.

But such comparisons are not entirely fair. While the Cagiva-Ducati F1 Montjuich is a production motorcycle (200 will be produced in 1986, only 10 of which will be sold in the United States), it's not street-legal here, nor in most other countries. Its exhaust, while meeting competition standards, is simply too loud. Instead, Cagiva has produced a homologation special, a machine with minimal street equipment that can serve as a basis for its racing programs. But unlike some other competition machines, the Montjuich is delivered with lights and an electric starter, and is available from your Cagiva dealer.

Anyone who buys a Montjuich gets, in the steel and alloy of the bike itself, a history of Ducati's racing milestones over the past few years. Ducati first housed special 600cc Pantah engines in monoshock trellis frames for

GP-size Michelin racing tire required the aluminum swingarm to be wider than the standard F1 arm; an offset countershaft sprocket moved the chainline out to clear the tire. As with all well-set-up roadracers, rear-wheel lockup with the twin-piston, floating-disc brake requires a hard push on the pedal.

A pair of 40mm Dell'Orto accelerator-pump-equipped carbs meters fuel to the Montjuich's engine. Throttle effort is suprisingly light, but the reasonable effort has been purchased with longish throttle travel.

Italian championship events (where they trounced GPz550-engined Bimotas), and for international TT2 races (production-based 350cc two-strokes versus 600cc four-strokes). Later, bored and stroked to 748cc, Pantah engines were used in the same frame for TT1 and endurance races, again with success.

While the Ducati factory was wobbling on its last fiscal legs in 1984, the 750 F1, a street version of the TT1 racer, was announced. It would use a cooking version of the 750 race engine, with valve sizes the same as the 600 street engine, and mild cam timing; and the frame would be altered slightly to provide more rake and trail for slower steering, and slightly different tube placement for better engine access.

Despite Ducati's plan, the F1 nearly remained a fantasy, lost in the financial collapse of the Bologna-based producer of V-Twins. But Cagiva rescued and reorganized Ducati, and produced the F1 in the thousands, instead of the hundreds Ducati originally intended. We tested one in Italy (September, 1985, issue), and found it a wonderfully fun, if not lightning fast, 750 sportbike.

But the F1, no matter how much fun, was a somewhat lackluster performer compared to its racing ancestors.

And while Ducati may have been willing to settle for that, Cagiva wasn't. The Castiglioni brothers, owners of Cagiva-Ducati, had already enticed Ducati V-Twin designer Dr. Fabio Taglioni from retirement to work on engine improvements. Surely, he could find more power in the 750 Pantah engine.

For the Montjuich he did. The 90-degree V-Twin Pantah engine, with two valves per cylinder, may seem somewhat dated, but it has responded well to Taglioni's hot-rodding. Re-done cylinder heads now use 750cc-size valves: 41mm intakes and 35mm exhausts, compared with the 37.5mm and 33.5mm poppets on the 1985 F1 engine. New camshafts hold these valves open 15 percent longer, while intake and exhaust overlap has more than doubled, from 67 to 137 degrees. Carburetor size is up, as well, with 40mm Dell'Orto pumpers replacing the 36mm units on the F1. The exhaust system, merely loud on the F1, has been replaced by a Morselli "full race" 2-into-1 equipped with a baffle a young boy could pass his fist through.

These changes have certainly increased power; an Italian magazine measured 75 horses at a Montjuich's rear wheel, a good number for a Four, a nearly incredible

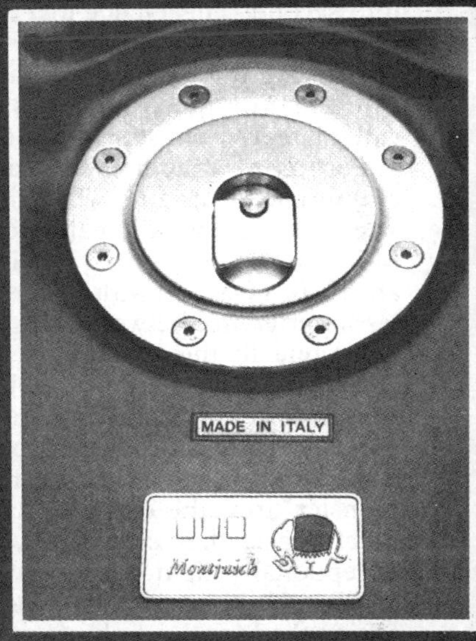

Front brake uses Brembo floating discs and four-piston calipers, the same as those used last year on Eddie Lawson's Yamaha GP bike. Two·fingers provide all the pressure necessary to howl the front tire.

Each of the 200 Montjuichs comes with a nameplate for display of its production number; our test bike, one of the first built, was equipped with the plate, but not the number.

PHOTO BY RICH CHENET

MONTJUICH

figure for a 750 Twin.

But numbers don't tell about this engine's exceptional character. Despite its extreme cam timing, it will pull from 2000 rpm at partial throttle openings. At 4000 it runs stronger and will tolerate full throttle. Then, from 6500 rpm to the 9000-rpm redline and even 1000 rpm beyond, it accelerates truly *hard*, singing a song of power as pure and deep as the one played by Marco Luchinelli's Daytona Battle-of-the-Twins-winning Ducati. The Montjuich bellows through the gears, with a sharp, metallic thunder, like a blacksmith hammering a glowing piece of steel thousands of times a minute. And on the overrun, it belches a hollow, haunting rasp that makes you understand why people once paid good money for recordings of four-stroke racing bikes at speed.

This 750 Twin will tolerate 10,000 rpm for brief bursts of acceleration, its mechanically positive desmodromic valve gear ensuring that valve float is non-existent. This engine will pull the front wheel up a foot with a hard shift into second. This engine loves to rev, but does so without feeling particularly peaky.

Carrying the engine is a chassis that's at least as special. The Montjuich's frame is right off of the F1, fabricated largely from straight tubes, with the engine acting as part of the structure. The gas tank is handmade from aluminum sheet, and, where it fits between the rider's knees, is considerably narrower than the rear tire. The Montjuich, while a racer, cradles its rider more comfortably than a GSX-R, with more seat-to-footpegs room and less interference between rider and gas tank.

Unique to the Montjuich are truly special Marvic wheels, with cast centers that bolt to Akront aluminum rims. These exceptionally wide rims carry Michelin racing tires in 500cc Grand Prix sizes—4.6 inches wide in the front, and over 7 inches for the back. But despite the monster tires, the overall package is tiny, not all that much bigger than some 250s, and, at 367 pounds dry, exceptionally light. Even the addition of turnsignals (rubber plugs cover turnsignal mounting holes in the fairing the Montjuich shares with the regular F1) and an effective muffler would still see this motorcycle weighing 50 pounds less than a GSX-R750. Stripped of electric starter and street gear for competition, it could easily approach 300 pounds.

So what does all this hardware yield in terms of a riding experience? The engine was every bit as impressive as described, but we initially found the chassis disappointing. The combination of the exceptionally wide, low-profile tires, the narrow handlebars and the unusually large amount of trail (5.2 inches, compared with under 4 inches for most Japanese sportbikes) made steering very heavy at high speed and imprecise when going slow. Once we got more familiar with the bike, the handling felt better; and during testing at Willow Springs, the harder the Montjuich was ridden, the better it seemed to respond to steering input.

Suspension, however, was less than satisfactory. In our first laps at Willow, both wheels chattered over the small bumps that can be found on that track, bumps that disappear under the more-compliant suspensions of a Honda VFR or Suzuki GSX-R. A single adjustment knob on the Montjuich's Marzocchi rear shock was able to render the rear suspension useless with either no perceptible damping, or so much of it that the rear end was essentially rigid. Fortunately, an intermediate position allowed the

The 2-into-1 exhaust system is stamped "RISERVATO COMPETIZIONE," and the sound that comes out confirms it. Running at full throttle, the Montjuich sounds more like a V-Eight racecar than a motorcycle. The engine is very smooth until 8000 rpm, but above that speed it buzzes the footpegs.

rear end to work better, if not perfectly.

Not so with the Forcelle Italia fork; even with all adjustments set to their minimum values, excess friction and stiffness prevented the front wheel from accurately tracking the pavement. Steve Stortz, the U.S. distributor of F.I. forks, tells us this is atypical; whatever the cause, the fork on our test bike was simply not up to current standards.

We were able to improve upon some aspects of the Montjuich's behavior a bit later in the test, while prepping the bike for competition in the La Carrera, a point-to-point roadrace held in Mexico (see "La Carrera," pg. 48). We replaced the standard Michelin tires with slightly narrower, DOT-approved Michelin Hi-Sports (120/70-16 front, 160/80-16 rear). This change improved the steering, reducing both the turning effort and the Montjuich's tendency to stand up while braking into a corner. The taller rear tire and a change from a 40-tooth to a 38-tooth rear sprocket allowed the Montjuich to reach an impressive 145 mph on the La Carrera's long straights, with equally impressive stability. Still, less-conservative steering geometry would likely sacrifice little of that stability for even more responsive steering.

So in the end, the Montjuich is an impressive, soulful machine in search of a clear mission. It's best suited as a Battle-of-the-Twins racer; it would require little modification to be competitive in the GP class; and if allowed in the stock class, it should easily dominate. The idea of street riding the Montjuich is tempting; but the anti-social exhaust note and the lack of paperwork necessary for legal registration render that proposition more than a little impractical.

Perhaps like the Rolling Stones, the Montjuich's true home is in the past, in a 1960s setting where it could run with side-piped Corvettes and open-exhaust GTOs. Certainly, the safe and sane and noise-controlled Eighties will restrict it to closed-circuit use.

But the Montjuich also points to the future, and to Cagiva's commitment to the Ducati V-Twin engine. Improvements such as the larger valves and refined carburetion will soon be incorporated into the street-going Cagiva-Ducati Paso, a machine that promises to have some of the Montjuich's out-of-the-past character without offending present-day sensibilities.

But no matter; the Montjuich is its own reason for being, and the song it sings at 9000 rpm is so sharp and so pure that it needs no other excuse. ◙

SPECIFICATIONS

GENERAL

List price	$8800
Importer	Cagiva North America
	20030 S. Normandie Ave.
	Torrance, CA 90502
Customer service phone	(213) 538-9337
Warranty	none

CHASSIS

Weight:	
Tank empty	367 lb.
Tank full	396 lb.
Weight distribution, front/rear, percent:	
Tank empty	47.0/53.0
Tank full	47.9/52.1
Fuel capacity	4.8 gal.
Wheelbase	56.0 in.
Rake/trail	28°/5.2 in.
Handlebar width	23.2 in.
Seat height	30.0 in.
Ground clearance	4.8 in.
GVWR	na
Load capacity (tank full)	na

DRIVETRAIN

Engine	air-cooled, four-stroke V-Twin
Bore x stroke	88.0 x 61.5mm
Displacement	748cc
Compression ratio	9.3:1
Claimed power	na
Claimed torque	na
Valve train	sohc, two valves per cyl., desmodromic operation, shim adj.
Valve adjustment intervals	3000 mi. or every race
Carburetion	(2) 40mm Dell'Orto
Air filter	none
Lubrication	wet sump
Oil capacity	3.6 qt.
Starter	electric
Primary drive	gear
Clutch	multi-plate, dry
Final drive	520 O-ring chain
Sprocket sizes	15/40
Gear ratios, overall:1	
1st	13.15
2nd	9.02
3rd	7.01
4th	5.65
5th	5.08

ELECTRICAL

Electrical power	300w
Battery	12v, 14ah
Headlight	60/55 halogen

SUSPENSION/TIRES/BRAKES

Front suspension:	
Manufacturer	Forcelle Italia (Ceriani)
Tube diameter	40mm
Wheel travel	5.1 in.
Adjustments	rebound damping, compression damping
Rear suspension:	
Manufacturer	Marzocchi
Type	single shock
Wheel travel	4.3 in.
Adjustments	rebound damping, spring preload
Wheels:	
Front	Marvic MT3.50 x 16
Rear	Marvic MT4.25 x 16
Tires:	
Front	12/60-16 Michelin racing intermediate (approx. equivalent to 120/80-16)
Rear	18/67-16 Michelin 1262A racing intermediate (approx. equivalent to 180/70-16)
Rear tire revs. per mi.	839
Brakes:	
Front	(2) 10.9 in. disc
Rear	9.1 in. disc

PERFORMANCE

ACCELERATION

Time to distance:	
¼ mi.	11.87 sec.
	@ 113.52 mph
Time to speed, sec.	
0–30 mph	1.5
0–40 mph	2.1
0–50 mph	2.7
0–60 mph	3.5
0–70 mph	4.4
0–80 mph	5.4
0–90 mph	6.8
0 100 mph	8.6
Top gear time to speed, sec.	
40–60 mph	4.4
60–80 mph	4.0

SPEED IN GEARS

Measured top speed	136 mph
Calculated at 9000 rpm redline:	
1st gear	49 mph
2nd gear	71 mph
3rd gear	92 mph
4th gear	114 mph
5th gear	127 mph
Engine speed at 60 mph	4260 rpm

FUEL MILEAGE

High/low/avg.	na
Avg. range inc. reserve	na

BRAKING DISTANCE

from 30 mph	29 ft.
from 60 mph	114 ft.

SPEEDOMETER ERROR

50 kph indicated	42 kph
100 kph indicated	89 kph

DUCATI LOVERS NEED NOT HAVE worried. Ever since Cagiva acquired that Bologna-based manufacturer of desmo engines and uncompromised sportbikes, Ducati loyalists have been concerned that the character of Cagiva-Ducati motorcycles would change, degenerating into the less sporting, even the ordinary.

Cagiva addressed those doubts at this year's Milan show with the unveiling of the 750 Paso. Named after the late Italian roadrace hero Renzo Pasolini (who rode for Aermacchi, Cagiva's corporate ancestor), the Paso uses a much-upgraded Ducati 750 Pantah V-Twin engine carried in an entirely new chassis, all enclosed in the most aerodynamic bodywork ever to grace a streetbike.

Engine modifications are designed to boost power while eliminating some long-standing consumer nitpicks. Bigger valves and revised cam timing pick the power up to 75 bhp at 9000 rpm, and throttle effort at long last is reduced to Japanese-bike levels by a push-pull linkage that allows the Dell'Orto carbs to use light return springs. A new, Japanese-made ignition gives a more-gradual spark-advance curve, smoothing power flow off idle; the current Pantah-engined bikes can be abrupt at low rpm as the timing suddenly advances 20 degrees.

But the engine changes are minor compared to those in the the chassis, which bears little resemblance to any Ducati, or even the original prototype Cagiva-Ducati Bimota built under commission (shown in the September, 1985, *Cycle World*); instead, the Paso is completely a product of Massimo Tamburini, former Bimota chief designer, now head of Cagiva's design studio. He sculpted the Paso around a set of very-low-profile, 16-inch Pirelli radials. Because these tires are very short, they allow Ducati's long V-Twin to be packaged close to the front of a long, low and narrow motorcycle, giving the forward weight bias needed for best handling. At 57.2 inches, the wheelbase helps to slow down the quick steering that could result from such a small front tire; those who have ridden the

prototype report that the Paso steers lightly with excellent stability. Handling should also be aided by the low overall weight: a claimed 373 pounds dry. Both front and rear suspensions use the best available components (a Marzocchi M1 fork in front, an Ohlins single shock in back), and both wheels can travel about 5.5 inches, enough for good ride quality but not so much as to compromise handling.

Many such balances have been sought with the Paso. The bodywork gives low drag with good engine cooling (twin oil coolers can be found embedded in the fairing sides), but the riding position is more reminiscent of the Interceptor's or FJ1100's than that of a racebike or of an old Ducati 900SS, and that may mean that chiropractors won't have much business from Paso owners. Even the windowless fairing design is intentional; the solid top of the fairing is low enough to look over while in a full tuck, and is stronger and lighter than a clear plastic bubble would be. Maintenance was considered in the design, as well; the rectangular-tube frame gives good engine access after the body panels are removed. In the end, the Paso seems a well-conceived, professional design offering plenty of flash and performance, but still meeting real-world needs.

A word of caution, however: The Paso shown in these photographs is very much a prototype, a showbike that we shanghaied for a few hours while it was in the U.S. during a Pirelli radial tire introduction. Production of Pasos isn't scheduled to begin until April, 1986, and they won't be available in the U.S. until at least the fall of 1986. Some details, such as the turn signals, will certainly have to change on the production model, and there is even talk of giving American Pasos a different name. Cagiva anticipates a price in the upper $4000 range, but that, too, is subject to the vagaries of manufacturing and exchange rates.

Still, however it may evolve during the next few months, the Paso is already strong evidence that there is nothing ordinary or unsporting about Cagiva motorcycles. ▣

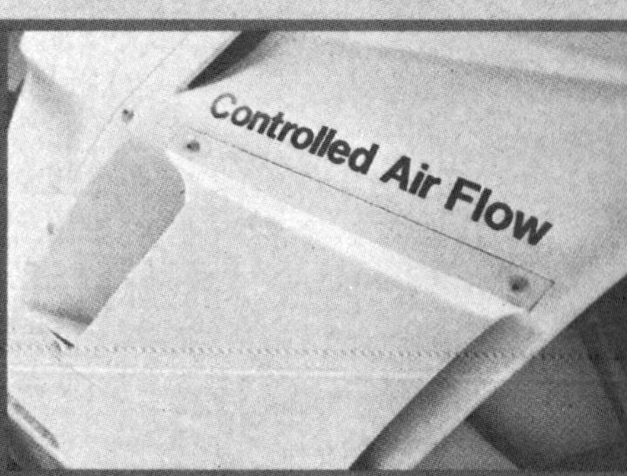

PASO
ARE ALIVE AND WELL IN VARESE

PHOTOS BY BRIAN BLADES

CAGIVA-DUCATI 750 PASO

From the unlikely marriage of a Duck and an elephant comes one of the world's truly fine sport motorcycles

FEW THINGS IN LIFE ARE BETTER THAN A FIRE-ENGINE-red Italian sportbike that's *right*. Sex, maybe, or Häagen-Dazs chocolate chocolate-chip. But not by much. And when an Italian sportbike is as red and as right as Ducati's newest corner-bender, the 750 Paso . . . well, as the beer commercial says, that's about as good as it gets.

And take our word for it: The Paso is indeed right. We found that out for ourselves by traveling to Italy, where we probed this intriguing machine's innermost workings, talked to the people responsible for its existence, and became the first journalists anywhere in the world to ride a Paso both on the racetrack and on public roads, racking up more than 500 miles on the very machine you see here. After all that, we can assure you that what you're looking at is the closest thing to a two-wheeled Ferrari you're likely to find, a bike that is exciting to look at, thrilling to ride, and just plain fun to be around.

Visually, the Paso's swoopy, all-enclosing bodywork lavishly coated in positively *electric* red paint captivates everyone who lays eyes on it. And functionally, it is the most delightful Ducati in eons, combining the tractable power and traditional virtues of Dr. Fabio Taglioni's beloved V-Twin engine with an ultra-modern chassis that is one of the most magnificent ever to come out of Italy.

In other words, this is not last year's Ducati dolled up in a new red dress; this Ducati is unlike any other that has gone before it. For one thing, it is the first all-new Ducati produced since the acquisition of that company by Cagiva in 1984. So officially, it is the *Cagiva*-Ducati 750 Paso.

What's more, the only part of the Paso that has been designed and developed at the Ducati factory in Bologna is the 750cc engine, which is essentially an upsized and refined version of the desmodromic-valve, 90-degree V-Twin that first saw the light of day in the 500 Pantah back in 1979. The entire remainder of the Paso is the brainchild of Massimo Tamburini and his design team stationed in Rimini, about an hour down the road from Bologna. Chief of design for Cagiva since 1984, Tamburini formerly was a partner in Bimota, the exotic-bike builders also located in Rimini. So if you think you detect a slight aroma of Bimota wafting through the Paso's chassis, you're probably right.

That may come as a surprise to you, but not to Gianfranco and Claudio Castiglioni, owners of the ever-

750 PASO

growing Cagiva empire. Early last year, the brothers Castiglioni charged Tamburini with the design of an entirely new Ducati sportbike, giving him free reign to do whatever he so desired with everything except the V-Twin engine. He responded by designing precisely the sort of machine he'd build for his own enjoyment, even naming it in memory of his longtime friend, the late Renzo "Paso" (pronounced PAW-so) Pasolini, the GP roadrace star killed in a racing accident in 1973. Tamburini loaded his "dreambike," as he affectionately calls it, with the cost-is-no-object stuff of which a motorcycle designer's fantasies are made: gorgeous aluminum forgings, the highest-quality hardware, and some of the most beautifully machined and flawlessly crafted componentry one could imagine. In fact, the Paso has such a custom-built flavor that some insiders are already calling it a "production-line Bimota."

Still, for many people, the most memorable aspect of the Paso is its stunning, ultra-modern appearance. When Tamburini was designing the sleek, deeply sculptured bodywork that fully encloses the engine and frame, his main objective was styling; but, since future plans call for the Paso to be liquid-cooled, heat control also was in the back of his mind. And as we found, the full bodywork does a superb job of diverting engine heat away from the rider.

But that pretty much tells the story of the Paso. It's not just another pretty face; it's a wonderfully functional motorcycle that flat *works*. After a full day on the Misano race circuit and another day playing in the rugged mountains to the east of Rimini, we came away thoroughly enchanted with what Tamburini has crafted.

We were most impressed with the handling, which was so crisp, so precise, so confidence-inspiring that we found ourselves charging corners downright *aggressively* within a few minutes of saddling up the bike for the very first time. The Paso reacts immediately to the rider's input and is

A ZANNI
DUCATI
Controlled Air Flow
DESMO
750 PASO

All major electrical components are located on a single, aluminum panel beneath the Paso's dual seat.

Carburetion is via a single Weber two-barrel instead of the dual Dell'Ortos usually found on Ducati V-Twins. The Weber is of the type used on numerous sportscars, including the Ferrari Dinos of the Sixties and Seventies.

Massimo Tamburini

On Pasos and Paganini

MASSIMO TAMBURINI IS A HAPPY MAN. But at the moment, his happiness isn't obvious. Surrounded by engineers and workmen, a frowning Tamburini is twisting and turning an engine-mounting bracket, trying to make it fit between Paso frame and Ducati engine. It won't. The frame and bracket are the first made from production tooling, and Tamburini doesn't force their mating. Unlike a mechanic, who would expect parts to fit, Tamburini isn't too surprised to find some that don't.

Drawings are consulted. The boss on the frame isn't correctly located; a frame jig must be changed.

Tamburini watches while the engineers add other parts to the frame, while the skeleton and ligaments and musculature of a Paso, the first to be made from production parts, take shape on the low work table. This testing of production tooling is the last stage of a project dear to Tamburini, the creation of his dream-bike. The project has taken little more than 14 months, and will continue for a few more while final problems are solved. It's this project, and his relationship with Cagiva, that has given Tamburini his glow of satisfaction.

Tamburini is hardly new to creating motorcycles. He is the "ta" in Bimota (named for its founders: BIanchi, MOrri, and TAmburini), and until a few years ago, was the chief designer there. The walls of his house are lined with photos of machines he has sculpted: the Kawasaki-engined Bimota KB1 and KB2 that had obvious influence on Kawasaki's Ninjas; the Honda-powered HB1; the swoopy, Suzuki-engined bikes whose reflection can be seen in the Yamaha FJ1100. There are racing photos, as well, some of Randy Mamola on the Bimota-Yamaha that nearly won the Daytona 250 race and, later that season, launched Mamola's GP career.

It was racing that led Tamburini away from Bimota, to the Gallina-Suzuki GP team, to experiments with exotic materials and chassis designs. That lasted only a year, until the Castiglionis, the owners of Cagiva, enticed him back to street motorcycle design.

Their methods of persuasion are evident. While Cagiva is located near the Swiss-Italian border in Varese, and Ducati centrally placed in Bologna, Tamburini's roots and family are in Rimini, on Italy's Adriatic coast. Rather than ask Tamburini to relocate, Cagiva built a design studio for him in this bright Italian resort.

But not just any studio: a motorcycle fabricator's dream. A few offices, complete with drawing boards, quite eager to change direction, yet it is extremely stable and always feels firmly planted. No matter if it's speeding along in a straight line or heeled way over in a turn, it feels like it's on outriggers. And unless the Paso is absolutely at its maximum lean angle—which, as we learned at Misano, is substantial—it allows you not just to change lines in a corner, but literally to "drive around" in the turn at will.

Tamburini's cantilever-style frame is responsible for much of this handling magnificence. Fabricated of square-section, chrome-molybdenum steel tubing, it is both light and rigid, and employs the engine as a stressed chassis member. His choice of steering geometry combines the light feel provided by an unusually steep (25-degree) head angle, with the directional stability imparted by an average amount (103mm) of trail.

Doing their part for the Paso's fine handling are high-quality suspension components, consisting of a flex-free Marzocchi M1R fork up front, and a single Ohlins shock at the rear. The damping-adjustable Ohlins works through a beefy aluminum swingarm and a forged aluminum linkage that uses sealed needle bearings at all pivot points.

Nevertheless, a sizable part of the chassis' ability to amaze is owed to its extremely low-profile Pirelli MP7S radial tires—the first *pure* radials included as original equipment on a production motorcycle. The Pirellis de-liver an extraordinary amount of feel and feedback, while clinging to the road as though it were sheet metal and they were the world's biggest refrigerator magnets. The use of 16-inch wheels at both ends, in combination with the exceptionally light weight and unusually small outside diameter of these 60-series, short-sidewall radials, dramatically reduces the gyroscopic effect of the spinning wheels; thus, the Paso can be flicked over into a turn as abruptly and instantaneously as any full-size streetbike we've ever ridden.

Apart from the handling, the tires also contribute immensely to the Paso's remarkable braking. We were easily able to generate enough force with the Brembo front discs to lift the rear wheel off the pavement at moderate speeds without causing even a hint of front-tire squirm or squeal. Not only that, you can trail the Paso's brakes while entering—or even while in the midst of—a fast, hard turn, and the bike won't try to sit up and run toward the outside of the turn. To some extent, this is the by-product of intelligent steering geometry and a low center of gravity, but the Pirelli people insist that much of it is due to the design of their radial tires. Whatever the cause, it makes fast cornering almost absurdly easy.

What's just as impressive is that the Paso offers such fine racetrack/sport-riding behavior without seriously detract-

open into a sunlit room behind, a room large enough to hangar an airliner. The walls are white, the floor immaculate, polished concrete. A few low, white dividers define the room: here a new milling machine; there a large, expensive lathe; over in the corner, a welding station with the best heli-arc equipment. A few motorcycles can be found in the front—Cagivas and Ducatis with styling modifications grafted on, a half-finished (and abandoned) chassis design for the big Ducati V-Twin. So much open space remains that 50 people could work here without ever bumping elbows. Instead, there are five: Tamburini, engineers Brutti and Paranti, and two machinists/fabricators.

These five are creating Cagiva-Ducati's future, with Tamburini clearly setting the course. The design procedure is a bit different from that followed by Japanese companies. There were no preliminary styling sketches of the Paso; as explained by Paranti, "the design comes right from Mr. Tamburini's head."

First come the mechanicals: A complete rolling chassis is done on the drawing board, and then quickly fabricated in the shop. Only then do the styling studies begin, with three-dimensional mockups of bodywork, in fiberglass, plaster or wood, fitted to the chassis. These are perfected to suit Tamburini's eye, and those of his clients: Gianfranco and Claudio Castiglioni. Only they can veto a Tamburini design. After approval, a running prototype is built. Testing then can lead to quickly implemented modifications, for better ergonomics, or aerodynamics, or handling.

Tamburini's love of quality and order are as evident on the Paso as in the spacious, uncluttered workshop. "We study every part of a new design—wheels, brakes, frames, even screws. There can be no random screwheads sticking out, no ugly joints." He points with pride to the Paso's refined rear axle and its eccentric adjusters, to the recessed Allen screws holding footpeg brackets, to the top triple-clamp and forged handlebars that are beautiful in their simplicity, not hidden behind plastic vanity covers. He's particularly pleased with the single panel under the seat that holds all important electrical components neatly arranged, easily accessible.

But Tamburini isn't satisfied with motorcycles as stationary garage art; motorcycles are meant to be ridden. During our visit, he took us on a ride on "his" road, a road magical in its deceit. Every third corner unexpectedly decreases in radius, seemingly regardless of direction of travel. The surface is at best rough, at worst crossed with sudden drops of several inches. This road demonstrated two things: First, that Tamburini is a very good, and quick, rider, and second, that the Paso's suspension and handling had to be outstanding to meet this standard.

But what of the future, of the bikes that will follow the Paso? Already, Tamburini's next project is underway, a sport-touring Ducati to compete with the BMW K100RS/RT. He thinks that its streamlining should completely enclose the engine as well, but Claudio Castiglioni doesn't, so the bodywork will be slightly more traditional than the Paso's. Its engine will be the enlarged, liquid-cooled version of the Paso 750's currently under development in Bologna, and fitted with shaft drive for this application. An interesting project, but still a very long way from production.

As Tamburini charts the near future of Cagiva-Ducati for us, he is clearly anxious for further updated Ducati engines. He has designed a chassis that sets new standards for the Japanese to aim for, and he clearly wishes for an engine that would erase any deficit of the Paso relative to four-cylinder 750s. Tamburini even admits that, while he appreciates Twins, a Four is his ideal. To explain why, he takes us over to an FZ750 sitting in a corner, a friend's bike that has been fitted with a 4-into-1 exhaust. "This makes power like an electric motor," he says, and starts the FZ. He blips the thottle, and is answered with a rippling howl. "Ah, that is *music*," Tamburini says with emotion as he mimes the drawing of a bow across a violin, "Paganini . . .."
                                                                    —*Steve Anderson*

Dr. Taglioni

Designer of "difficult bicycles"

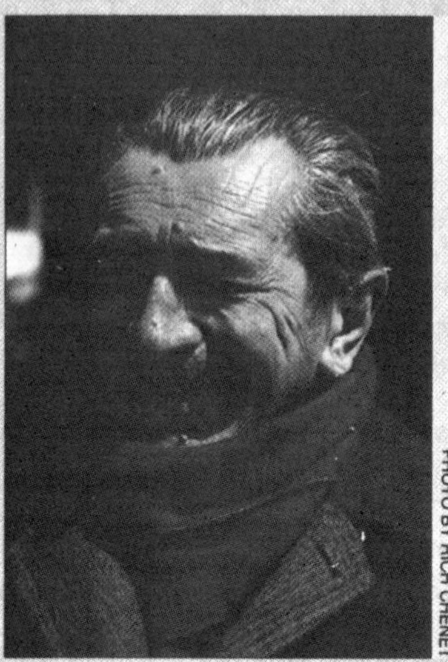

M R. FABIO TAGLIONI SITS QUIETLY IN THE MEET-
ing room in Bologna, smiling at us. He's
come to talk, to answer our questions, but his
English is no better than our Italian. The language
skills of Ducati's public-relations woman falter when
technical terms are used, so we just sit, matching
smiles with Dr. Taglioni.

Finally, we are joined by Mr. Sandro Rubbini, an
engineer and linguist; and Dr. Taglioni, the father of
so many Ducati engines since 1954, can now talk
about his latest 750cc version of the Pantah engine, as
used in the Paso.

"There are many refinements; larger valves and
ports, improved ignition, better valve guide materials,
increased oil flow for better cooling, and the Weber
carburetor. The Weber is important. For one thing, it
gives us access to Weber's great experience in meeting
automotive emissions standards. It is also a good alli-
ance for the future, as Weber is working on electronic
fuel injection, and we are very interested in fuel
injection."

Engineer Rubbini, whose own responsibility is seeing the Paso homologated for European and American markets, likes the new carburetor as well. "The
Weber is more difficult to calibrate initially, and we
are newcomers at this," he says, "but it is much more
precise when you are finished."

Dr. Taglioni continues, "The cam profile for the
Paso is new also, at least for production. The cam was
developed for the 600cc TT2 racing bike several years
ago, but we found it gives good results in the larger
engine. With the Paso, we have 67 horsepower at the
rear wheel, maybe 75 at the crankshaft."

Taglioni goes on to discuss new projects at Ducati.
"We must water-cool the Pantah engine. In city driving it will stay cooler, but more important are homologation requirements—water-cooling will help us meet
the noise laws. Also, it is easier to keep down pollu-
tion with smaller differences in temperature within
the engine." Earlier, Dr. Taglioni had told how he had
designed the Pantah engine with liquid-cooling in
mind; there is already a boss on the cases where the
water pump can be placed.

"And, yes, we are studying four-valve heads for the
Pantah," he continues. "I can't say much more, but
they do use desmodromic valve gear. We must test
many things and then we will see."

Taglioni has been calm and impassionate so far, but
he comes to life when we ask him about the direction
motorcycle design is taking. He answers with a long
discourse in Italian, speaking with more energy, even
with some bitterness on this subject. Rubbini is hard-
pressed to keep up the translation. "Progress is to
make a good motorcycle that is not expensive. The
Japanese make bad policy because they fight each
other. Every day, the Japanese study a new accessory
for motorcycles—but there *are* no accessories for motorcycles. The Japanese are building cars. Motorcycles are something else, something completely
different.

The Doctor pauses, then looks at us directly. "The
Japanese motorcycle companies want to make an easy
car; *I* want to make a difficult bicycle."

—Steve Anderson

ing from its all-around streetability—which is, after all, its
primary mission. As we found on the streets and highways
in and around Rimini, the Paso's ride is a pleasant compromise—not taut enough to be called harsh, not soft enough
to be termed plush. It's just . . . *nice.* The seat is contoured
to allow serious knee-draggers to act out their finest Lucky
Lucchinelli impersonations; but it's also fairly thick, well-
padded and smartly shaped, and doesn't turn a long ride
on the open road into an exercise in self-abuse. And while
the critical seat/bar/peg relationship is configured for competent sport riding, it allows decent long-range comfort, as
well. Overall, in fact, there is a certain degree of similarity
between the Paso's ergonomics and those of some Japanese sportbikes, Honda's VFR750 in particular.

But engine-wise, there are no similarities whatsoever
between the Paso's V-Twin and the multi-cylinder power-
houses found in Japanese sportbikes. The Paso will, however, have the most powerful 750cc Ducati engine that has
ever been street-legal in this country. The engine is essentially in the same state of tune as the current 750 F1 motor,
but with more-restrictive intake and exhaust systems to
meet U.S. regulations. Of course, it retains the desmodromic valve system pioneered by Dr. Taglioni, with the
bigger valves, more-radical cams and higher compression
ratio that first appeared on the F1 this year. The ignition
system provides a smooth, gradual advance curve rather
than the abrupt, two-step advance used previously, and an
improved, dual-circuit oiling system better lubricates the
cams and followers while also aiding engine cooling.

Really, the only big news in the engine department is
the adoption of a single, automotive-style Weber two-barrel downdraft carburetor in place of the usual pair of
sidedraft Dell'Ortos or Bings used on other Ducks. The
Weber sits high in the vee of the cylinders atop a long
intake manifold, under a large airbox that occupies a
hollowed-out area at the front of the Paso's 4.8-gallon gas
tank. Ducati chose this carb for a number of reasons, not
the least of which is Weber's vast store of expertise in the
rather knotty area of exhaust emissions.

That may be so, but there was no evidence of anyone's
carburetion expertise on the Paso we rode. It was more
than willing to sputter and wheeze on certain occasions,
usually when the throttle was whacked open from lower
revs. But Taglioni & Co. assured us that they were on top
of the problem, and that the Webers on production Pasos
would carburate as crisply and cleanly as the carbs on
current Ducatis, if not more so.

Because of those carburetion glitches—and a badly worn
clutch that chattered violently when engaged under full
throttle—decent quarter-mile launches were impossible; so
our best quarter-mile ET was only 12.9 seconds. Most of
the time, though, the Weber carb worked properly, allowing the engine to perform up to par. We clocked a respect-
able top speed of 131 mph, and we expect that a production Paso will click through the quarter-mile lights
somewhere in the mid-12-second area.

Typical of Ducati V-Twins, the engine has a flat-as-a-
board, completely usable power curve, with no discern-
able bumps or dips anywhere between 2000 or 2500 rpm
and the 9000-rpm redline. When you want to go faster,
you just open the throttle. And that, along with the Paso's
responsive steering and crisp handling, allows a moder-
ately fast ride on a twisty backroad to be about as effortless
an affair as you could ask for. Only when you want that

CONTINUED ON PAGE 47

LUCKY DUCATI

This motorcycle holds Ducati's 8-valve future

BY STEVE ANDERSON

IF...IF IT HAD BEEN ELIGIBLE FOR THE DAYTONA 200, IT would have qualified sixth, behind Honda's Bubba Shobert but ahead of Yamaha's Jimmy Filice. If it had been in the Superbike class, its trap speed of 165.44 mph would have made it Daytona's seventh-fastest Superbike, as fast as the Yoshimura GSX-R750 of eventual second-place finisher Satoshi Tsujimoto, and only six mph down on Wayne Rainey's winning VFR750. If it could have run in Sunday's main event, it would have been tested against more-equal competition. Its rider, Marco

Marco Luccinelli rode the Ducati Eight-Valve to win Daytona's Battle of the Twins race.

PHOTO BY RICH CHENET

PHOTOS BY DAVID DEWHURST

DUCATI

The front cylinder head says it all: "Desmo 4V DOHC."
Above the head is the large water radiator that cools
this engine; below is the small oil radiator that assists.

A water pump has been grafted to the left side of the
Pantah engine cases, driven by the half-engine-speed
shaft that drives the cams. The plumbing in this first
prototype engine is complex and ugly, and will almost
certainly be simplified in later iterations.

Luchinelli, said that it came out of corners as "strong as an
FZ Yamaha Superbike." And all from a pair of four-stroke
cylinders—the ones that propelled this latest Ducati to victory in Daytona's Battle of the Twins event.

Like so many past Ducati racers, this new one has one
foot in Ducati's future, the other in Ducati's past. Its V-
Twin engine uses Pantah crankcases (the same as on all
current Ducati 650 and 750 engines) with a wider cylin-
der-stud pattern, carrying all-new liquid-cooled top ends.
Two 92mm pistons sweep through short, 64mm strokes to
displace a very oversquare 850cc.

Above those pistons are the heart of this engine: two
compact cylinder heads, each containing two camshafts,
four valves, and eight rocker arms, incorporating Ducati's

As on the Pantah engine, the new eight-valve Ducati uses belts to drive the cams. But all quantities have been doubled: Now there are two cams, four valves and eight rockers for each head. The throttle body in the front uses two electronic fuel injectors, one visible on the top, the other hidden on the opposite side.

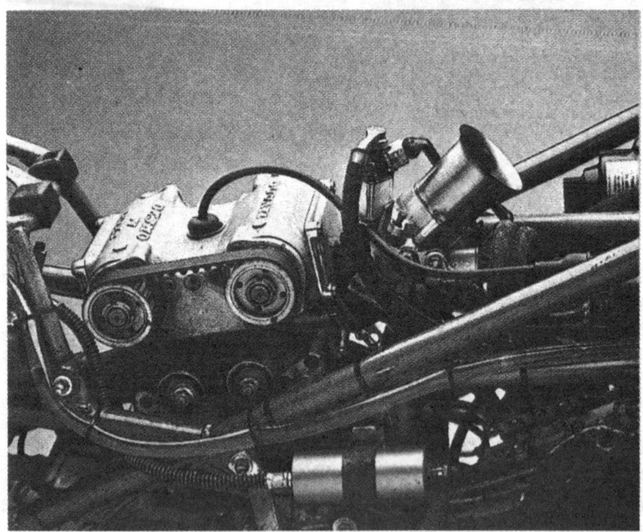

This Eight-Valve retains the narrowness typical of Ducati V-Twins. Like other Ducati engines, the width of the center cases is greater than on more densely packed V-Twins (Honda's Shadow engines, for example); this may be partially corrected with the new engine cases on later versions of this engine.

all-mechanical desmodromic valve actuation into a Cosworth-look head. One rocker pushes each valve open, and another rocker closes it. The only springs seen are small torsion items that insure proper valve sealing at idle.

These new four-valve heads bring Ducati into the 1980s, with a narrow, 40-degree angle between the valves that provides a compact combustion chamber. With desmodromic actuation and no large coil-spring pockets to wrap around the valve stems, the intake ports are free to take a straight run down to the valve heads. A Weber-Marelli electronic fuel-injection system (very loosely based on the unit used on F1 Ferraris) eliminates any problems with making carburetors work at strange angles of downdraft. Each throttle body is 47mm in diameter,

Ducati's latest engine retains desmodromic valve actuation, even though that means eight rocker arms have to find room in each head. The belt-driven cams each have four lobes, the smaller of which push valves open through slightly offset finger-follower-type rockers. The large lobes close valves via the lower set of rockers, the ones with the near-90-degree bend. Valve adjustment is by shim.

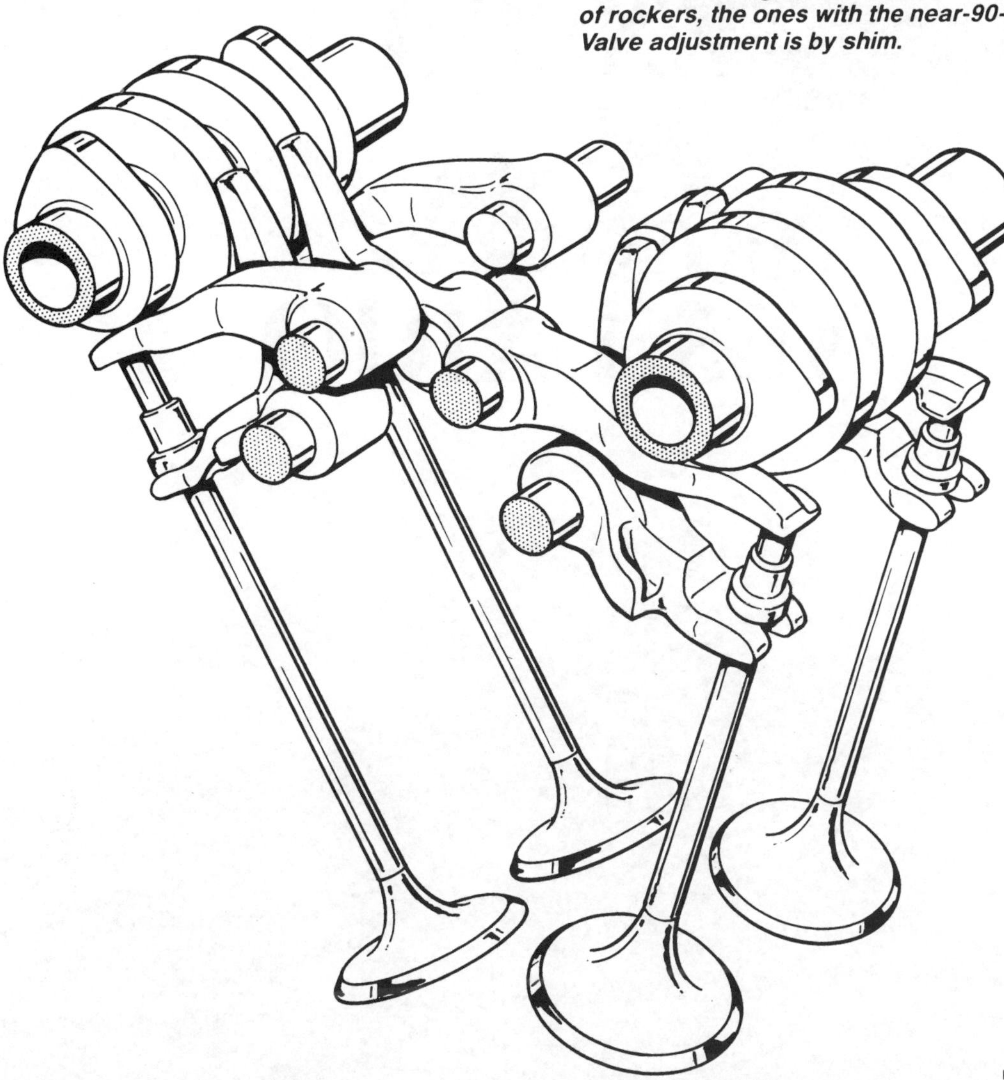

and fed by no less than two fuel injectors, probably because no standard automotive injector can flow enough fuel for this engine's powerful cylinders.

But the proof of this complex new Twin is its performance. According to Franco Farne, Development Chief of Ducati racing, this engine produces 120 horsepower *at the rear wheel*, at an engine speed astounding for an 850 Twin: 11,500 rpm. And the engine is safe to 12,000 rpm. But even more impressive is the spread of power. According to Luccinelli, "Power begins at 4000 rpm, and by 6000 rpm it is strong." Farne confirms this; he says that the engine's torque peak is at 7000 rpm, fully 4500 rpm below its power peak. This is no peaky screamer; this engine is a torque master.

Of course, in a project this new, not everything is perfect. At Daytona the fuel injection gave some problems, causing poor throttle response in the mid-range, and leaving the Ducati mechanics and Weber technician scratching their heads, wondering whether to make the injection leaner or richer. But Luccinelli is confident, knowing that this is the beginning, and that there are "many changes required. The fuel injection is new, but in one or two months it will be perfect."

Right now, the Ducati eight-valve is truly unique, the only one of its kind—but not for long. By May, it will have been followed by 25 replicas, replicas that will become eligible for Europe's Superbike class, replicas that will include some important improvements. New crankcases will incorporate six-speed gearboxes, and more metal around the cylinder bores, giving strength to grow even larger—to 920cc with just a bore enlargement, and perhaps to a full 1000cc with a stroke increase.

Later, after a season of racetrack testing, the eight-valve engine design will find its way into Cagiva/Ducati streetbikes. This engine is Ducati's future, and the people there are clearly excited by it. Perhaps Luccinelli tells it best: "We are developing this bike. Now we prefer this race (the Daytona Battle of the Twins)—the competition is not too strong. But later . . .."

And he smiles.

KAWASAKI EX500

VS.

MOTO GUZZI V65 LARIO

VS.

CAGIVA SS650

DICK LEANED ON THE COUNTER AT GARDNER CYCLES, gazing out the window at the Kawasaki EX500, doing very little to disguise his lack of interest in the motorcycle. "Ed and I don't see too many Japanese motorcycles around here," he said, and then turned a much more approving glance toward the two bikes parked beside the EX, a Moto Guzzi V65 Lario and a Cagiva/Ducati SS650.

"Around here" was the town of Gardner in northern Massachusetts. And Dick was right: There weren't many Japanese bikes around.

See, Gardner Cycle is the only motorcycle shop in town, and it doesn't carry Japanese bikes. Gardner is a throwback to an earlier time in motorcycle chronology, stuck somewhere between the era of British domination and the dawn of the Japanese age. Riders on big, four-cylinder Japanese rocketbikes flash by on the nearby interstate, hardly noticing the Gardner offramp, leaving the small New England town to its seemingly backward ways and backward motorcycles.

By and large, they sell Twins in Gardner, because that's what the riders there want—motorcycles like the Moto Guzzi and the Cagiva, simple machines that distill motorcycling back to a sport for riders and not technicians. And in Gardner, they measure the worth of a motorcycle by the pleasure it delivers on the road, not by the numbers printed in some California-based bike magazine. In short, Gardner is a one-bike-shop town where the motorcyclists have never quite figured out the attraction of the Japanese mystique.

But the Kawasaki is at least one Japanese bike that might be able to survive in Gardner. The EX500 fits the small-town mold for how a motorcycle should be. It appears to be Japanese only by some accident of geography, having more in common with bikes like the Guzzi and the Cagiva than it does with the multi-cylinder machines that more typically come from its country.

We made these observations while riding all three of these Twins on the backroads and highways of New England. That ride helped us understand what these very-similar-but-entirely-different bikes are all about. It also helped us learn quite a lot about the Northeast.

Now, just about the entire staff of CYCLE WORLD is made up of non-native Californians, a few of who have even lived in New England. And each staffer has, at one time or another, owned European metal. But too many years in La-La Land have dulled the memory. We don't keep change handy for eastern-style toll roads anymore; we tend to forget what annual freezing and thawing does to once-smooth asphalt.

At least the machinery is familiar enough. All three of these bikes are, of course, Twins, but the similarities don't stop there. All three are targeted somewhere between all-out sport hardware and more civil, touring-style bikes. If you had to give them a name, middleweight sport-tourers wouldn't be a bad one.

When it comes down to specifics, though, all three machines take different approaches to arriving at the same destination. The Guzzi is an overhead-valve, 90-degree V with a longitudinal crankshaft and shaft final drive. The pushrod engine is hardly on the leading technological edge, although it does have four valves per cylinder. The advantage of the Guzzi's layout is primarily in simplicity of maintenance—a decent mechanic can have a piston out of the engine and in his hand in about 20 minutes.

The Cagiva is the same tune played to a slightly different beat. It also is a 90-degree V-Twin, but with a transverse crank and chain drive. The Ducati motor is a single-overhead-cam, two-valve-per-cylinder model, and it's correspondingly harder to service than the Guzzi. The desmodromic valve system does away with valve springs, but while adjusting the valves isn't a mechanic's nightmare, it's at least an unpleasant dream.

Kawasaki's approach is a transverse vertical Twin with chain final drive. The EX's only high-tech twists are its four valves per cylinder and liquid-cooling, if you can still call such features high-tech. Rather, the Kawasaki is just a good, solid design, built around an engine that was originally used in the 454 LTD.

Despite their engine-configuration differences, all three bikes share a singularity of purpose. They weren't built to set new quarter-mile records, and they weren't made to emulate Eddie Lawson's latest GP bike. The Guzzi Lario, the Cagiva SS and the Kawasaki EX were made for the road. They were made for riding and for the enjoyment of the ride.

And it's on a long ride where you learn all about what makes this a very special breed of motorcycle. These are bikes you can't ride for just a few miles and hope to understand. You have to *experience* them for days before you come to terms with their way of doing things. It isn't so much what these motorcycles do that's important, but the way they make you *feel*.

The Guzzi, for example, lulls its rider down the road, playing a bass melody with the gentle loping of its motor. On the highway, the Lario loves to be shifted into high gear and have its thumbscrew-style cruise control locked just a crack above idle. The engine pulses smoothly, and vibration only raises its annoying head above 5000 rpm—and even then, it isn't the high-frequency buzzing that afflicts many four-cylinder motorcycles, but more of a soft shake.

The Ducati motor does its shaking at the other end of the rpm scale. In top gear, it snorts and rattles until you bring it up above 65 mph, where it then begins to smooth out and act more civilized. Both of these Italian bikes are geared tall and appreciate wide-open spaces where they can stretch their legs and *run*.

No matter what the speed, the Kawasaki's vibration level doesn't change much: It's always fairly smooth. The EX does have more of a buzz than a shake, but it's still no bother at all compared to what you feel on most modern sportbikes. The engine revs much more quickly than do those in the other Twins, and has the sound and feel of a small, responsive motor. But that's not surprising, considering that the Kawasaki has the smallest engine of the trio.

The EX500 also has the smallest chassis of the bunch. Compared to either of the V-Twins, the Kawasaki feels tiny, almost toy-like. Nevertheless, its seating position is more spread-out than those on any of the Japanese 600s; by FZ or Ninja standards, the EX has low footpegs and fairly high bars. The seat is rather low, however, so the rider's legs still are a bit confined. By comparison, the Cagiva is much more spread-out, giving the rider more or less the same amount of room as found on the "standard" motorcycles of the Seventies.

On the Lario, the seat-to-footpeg relationship is almost the same as on the Cagiva, but Moto Guzzi took the GP-racer approach to upper-body positioning. The handlebars are clip-ons that cant downward and rearward, putting the rider in a full tuck. Thus, the Guzzi has the least-comfortable rider positioning of the three for highway touring, only because so much of the rider's weight is on his hands.

And the amount of rider weight that's on the Guzzi's saddle isn't all that well cared-for, either. The Lario's seat is typically Italian—that is, hard, and shaped nothing at all like a *human* seat. It's wide, flat and has fairly sharp edges. It's not all that bothersome on a short ride, but by the time you get very far outside of even a small town the size of Gardner, the numbness in the nether regions starts getting more and more aggravating.

About the only good thing you can say about the Guzzi's seat is that it's better than the Cagiva's. While the contour of the SS's seat looks like it might not put anyone in the traction, the foam is absurdly dense. So once again, by the time you're ready to stop for dinner, you're also ready to eat standing up.

Voted most likely not to numb is the Kawasaki seat, with its medium-soft foam and well-rounded shape. It's not the Best Seat Ever In The History Of Things To Sit On, but it seems that way in contrast to those on the Cagiva and Guzzi.

Besides, New England roads aren't the type that keep you planted in the same part of the seat for hours on end. Variety is what this part of the country is all about. There's variety in roads, from superhighways to backroads that make the average motocross track seem smooth by com-

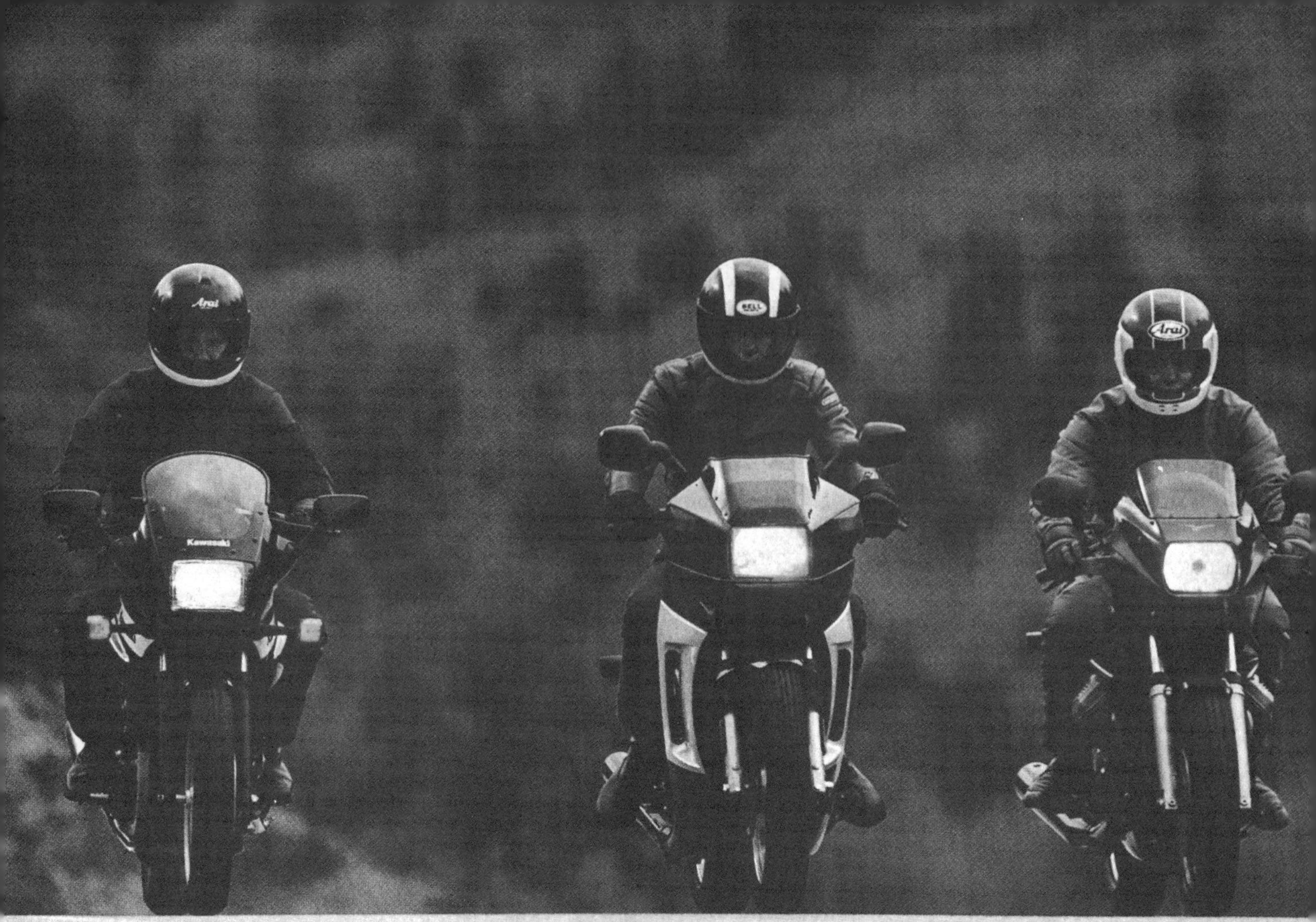
Arai
BELL
Arai
Kawasaki

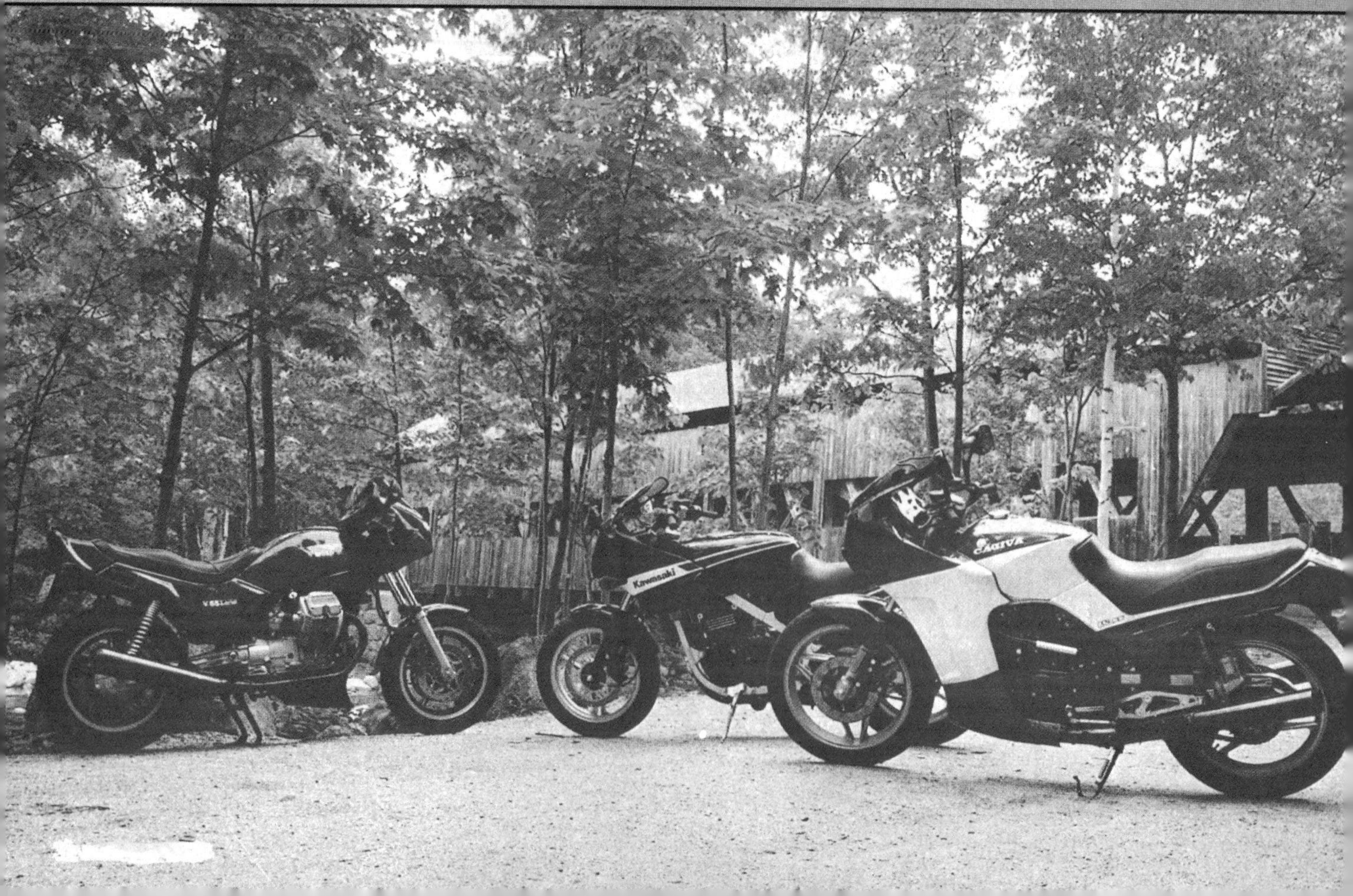
Kawasaki
CAGIVA

parison. And there's variety in weather; it seems that by the time you get your rain gear on, it's usually sunny and 90 degrees, and by the time you get your rain gear off, you can count on frigid rain.

We also discovered that the backroads of New England have an inordinately high policeman-to-motorcyclist ratio. No wonder riders in these parts scratch their heads and ask why anyone would want a 160-mph motorcycle. By the time you get any bike up to that kind of speed, you'll have gone through seven small towns and passed seven small-town police stations. There are sheriffs in Maine who have waited their whole lives for out-of-state motojournalists to try any of that road-test nonsense in *their* county.

Of course, even if all civil sense were suspended, scoring a 160-in-a-35 rap with these bikes isn't a realistic worry—although all three still are plenty capable of earning their riders a trip to the local traffic court. The Kawasaki is the most powerful of the lot, even if it's not the torquiest or the peakiest. Torque awards go to the Cagiva, which pulls from way down low with the satisfying, irregular beat that V-Twins do so well. After the initial power burst, however, the power of the Ducati engine tapers off. At high revs (meaning over 6000 rpm), the motor settles down, and more throttle is rewarded with more engine noise, but not necessarily more power.

Turn the Cagiva powerband upside-down and you've got the Guzzi powerband. Off the bottom, the Lario just plods lazily along, its heavy-flywheel feel doing little to excite. But once the engine climbs up over 6000, it starts to have some punch. In fact, the Guzzi will easily overrev its 7700-rpm redline unless the rider keeps a careful eye on the tach and shifts right on cue.

Still, even when the Guzzi's engine is kept near the top of its rather narrow powerband, the Lario won't run with the Kawasaki. Neither, for that matter, will the Cagiva. The EX has a revvy motor that is light on flywheel and heavy on acceleration, so it just runs away from the others when the need arises.

Another area where the EX excels is in suspension. We came to that conclusion in New Hampshire, which is—by our observation, at least—a suspension tester's worst fears and dream-come-true all rolled into one. That's another way of saying that the roads there are rough. It's as if some malevolent road-wrecker paced off every 20 feet of asphalt in the state and planted a land mine. So, as you can guess (and as riders in that area undoubtedly already know), a brisk pace on a motorcycle there means you spend a lot of time being airborne.

Obviously, such conditions do not favor the two European bikes, which are stiffly suspended. In the case of the Cagiva, road roughness also often results in an unsettling head shake. Along with being too stiff, the Marzocchi fork seems unable to cope with sudden loads; it doesn't even *try* to react to those volcano-class New Hampshire bumps. The rear end is better, although still on the stiff side, a condition made less tolerable by the SS650's hard seat.

Both ends of the Guzzi also are just as stiff. The Lario never does anything heart-stopping as a result, but the miles can begin to take their toll during a long ride on rough roads. But in all fairness, even the Kawasaki suspension is unable to deal with the roughest roads that New England has to offer. It's the only single-shocker of the

PHOTO BY RON LAWSON

bunch, and it's the smoothest-riding bike of the three, but streetbike suspension technology hasn't evolved enough to make those kinds of roads seem even remotely smooth.

Motorcycle technology has, however, progressed far enough that you shouldn't have to put up with things like the Cagiva's controls. Its grips are hard and shaped poorly, the levers are flat and uncomfortable, and the master cylinder for the hydraulic clutch doesn't allow full clutch disengagement. The Guzzi and the Kawasaki score much better in this department, both having good levers and grips—and clutches that work properly.

Likewise, the Kawasaki and the Guzzi both outperform the Cagiva in just about all braking maneuvers. Actually, the Cagiva's Brembo brakes get the job done, stopping the bike neither poorly nor superbly, but they demand that you squeeze *hard*. The Kawasaki unquestionably owns the best front brake of the bunch, despite having only one disc up there instead of two as the other machines do.

In terms of rear brakes, the Lario excels because of its integrated braking system. When you press on the Guzzi's rear brake pedal, you're also activating the front brake to a lesser degree. It's very difficult to lock up the Guzzi's rear wheel in a panic stop. Using the rear pedal only, the machine just slows, quickly and effectively. Admittedly, most experienced riders already know how to use the front and rear brakes in the proper proportions, but the Guzzi caters to less-experienced riders, as well.

Any rider, experienced or not, will appreciate the Guzzi's fine finish. Out of these three motorcycles—and perhaps out of *any* three bikes you care to mention—the Moto Guzzi is the attention-getter. The quality of its bright, arrest-me red paint is as near to perfect as a production bike is likely to get. And in its engine castings, as well as in the fit of all its component parts, the Guzzi is a

beautifully finished machine. The Cagiva also has a smooth, well-seen-to appearance that also allows it to be an attention-magnet—so long as it isn't parked near a crowd-pleaser like the Guzzi.

These two machines prove that fabled Italian craftsmanship is alive and living in more than one area of that country. In contrast, the Kawasaki goes almost unnoticed when in the company of the two Italian bikes. Its paint is quite good, but its overall finish is marred by all-too-visible seams and welds, causing the EX500 to lack the look and feel of an expensive motorcycle.

That's understandable, of course, considering that the Kawasaki *isn't* an expensive motorcycle, whereas its two Italian companions are. But on a strict, dollars-for-performance basis, the Kawasaki clearly comes out on top. It's the fastest, most powerful and most comfortable of the three, with the best ride and the best overall brakes—and it retails for just $2899, compared to the Guzzi's $5045 and the Cagiva's $4412.

But the folks in Gardner still probably wouldn't choose it over the Guzzi or the Cagiva. That's because those sorts of things just aren't that important to them. They'd point out that even though the Kawasaki is the most powerful in its class right now, it won't be in a year or so, and if you then want the fastest, you'll have to throw away a bike every year. All the other factors can be changed, they'd say. And by the time you've replaced the shocks and fiddled with this and that, what you wind up with isn't Cagiva's motorcycle or Moto Guzzi's motorcycle, it's *your* motorcycle. And that's worth the extra expense.

Good points, all. Still, though, for us, the Kawasaki is an easy, quantifiable winner. And you know what? We're willing to bet that Dick and Ed would like the Kawasaki, too. They just wouldn't admit it. ◘

The Cagiva wins the torque award amongst these three motorcycles, for it definitely has the most low-rpm power.

The carburetion on our Guzzi was way off the mark as delivered, but a local dealer was able to straighten it out free of charge.

Kawasaki's EX500 only has a single disc brake in the front and a drum in the rear, but still stops better than either of the two triple-disc Italian bikes.

	CAGIVA SS650 ALAZZURRA	KAWASAKI EX500	MOTO GUZZI V65 LARIO
GENERAL			
List price	$4412	$2899	$5045
Importer	Cagiva North America	Kawasaki Motors Corp. U.S.A.	Benelli/Moto Guzzi of North America
	700 W. 190th St.	P.O. Box 25252	1501 Caton Ave.
	Gardena CA 90248	Santa Ana, CA 92799	Baltimore, MD 21227
Customer service phone	(213) 538-9337	(714) 770-0400	(301) 646-3625
Warranty	12 mo./unlimited mi.	12 mo./unlimited mi.	12 mo./unlimited mi.
DRIVETRAIN			
Engine	air-cooled, four-stroke V-Twin	liquid-cooled, four-stroke Twin	air-cooled, four-stroke V-Twin
Bore x stroke	82.0 x 61.5mm	74.0 x 58.0mm	80.0 x 64.0mm
Displacement	650cc	498cc	643cc
Compression ratio	10.0:1	10.8:1	10.3:1
Claimed power	56 bhp @ 8400 rpm	59 bhp @ 9800 rpm	60 bhp @ 7800 rpm
Claimed torque	41 lb.-ft. @ 5800 rpm	34 lb.-ft. @ 8500 rpm	42 lb.-ft. @ 6600 rpm
Valve train	sohc, two valves per cyl., desmodronic operation, shim adj.	dohc, four valves per cyl., threaded adjusters	ohv, four valves per cyl., threaded adjusters
Valve adjustment intervals	3000 mi.	6000 mi.	1800 mi.
Carburetion	(2) 36mm Dell'Orto	(2) 34mm Keihin CV	(2) 30mm Dell'Orto
Clutch	multi-plate, dry	multi-plate, wet	single plate, dry
Final drive	chain	chain	shaft
CHASSIS			
Weight:			
Tank empty	446 lb.	400 lb.	407 lb.
Tank full	473 lb.	429 lb.	435 lb.
Fuel capacity	4.5 gal.	4.9 gal.	4.7 gal.
Wheelbase	56.9 in.	57.5 in.	57.8 in.
Rake/trail	29.5°/4.9 in.	29.5°/3.5 in.	na
Handlebar width	27.3 in.	24.9 in.	25.5 in.
Seat height	31.3 in.	30.5 in.	30.9 in.
Ground clearance	6.3 in.	4.9 in.	4.6 in.
GVWR	800 lb.	827 lb.	840 lb.
Load capacity (tank full)	323 lb.	398 lb.	405 lb.
TIRES/BRAKES			
Wheels			
Front	MT2.5 x18	MT2.15 x 16	MT2.15 x 16
Rear	MT3.0 x 18	MT2.50 x 16	MT2.50 x 16
Tires:			
Front	100/90 H18 Pirelli Phantom MT59	100/90-16 Bridgestone Exedra	100/90 V16 Pirelli Phantom MT29
Rear	120/80 H18 Pirelli Phantom MT58	120/90-16 Bridgestone Exedra	120/90 V16 Pirelli Phantom MT28
Rear tire revs. per mi.	794	834	843
Brakes:			
Front	(2) 10.2 in. disc	(1) 11.0 disc	(2) 10.6 in. disc
Rear	10.2 in. disc	drum	9.1 in. disc
PERFORMANCE			
Acceleration:			
Time to distance:			
¼ mi.	13.52 sec. @ 96.80 mph	12.99 sec. @ 101.98 mph	13.86 sec. @ 97.70 mph
Time to speed, sec.			
0-60 mph	5.0	4.2	5.2
Top gear time to speed, sec.			
40-60 mph	4.6	5.0	5.3
60-80 mph	5.4	5.8	7.0
SPEED IN GEARS			
Calculated at redline:	9000 rpm	11,000 rpm	7700 rpm
1st gear	44 mph	44 mph	49 mph
2nd gear	64 mph	64 mph	66 mph
3rd gear	83 mph	82 mph	84 mph
4th gear	103 mph	101 mph	102 mph
5th gear	118 mph	118 mph	120 mph
Engine speed at 60 mph	4580	4930	3850
FUEL CONSUMPTION			
High/low/avg	65/42/55 mpg	67/45/58 mpg	55/38/50 mpg
Avg. range inc. reserve	248 mi.	279 mi.	230 mi.

CAGIVA

WHEN MORE THAN A YEAR PASSES BETWEEN THE APpetizer and the main course, you can build up a powerful appetite. And when the appetizer is a motorcycle as promising and as tantalizing as the pre-production Ducati Paso we rode for our September, 1986 issue, the production-bike main course had better be *damned* good.

After all, the translation from prototype hopeful to production-line reality has been known to cook the flavor out of many a fine motorcycle design. So, that hand-built Paso we rode in Italy last year could have been misleading; it could have been faster, lighter and better-handling than anything the company was able to sell on a mass-produced basis. On the other hand, a year is plenty of time to pick the bugs out of the stew, to fix the few complaints we had about what was otherwise an impressive, captivating package.

For those of you who missed the opening act, the 750 Paso is Cagiva's top-of-the-line sportbike, a street-legal adventure in styling and performance. It's also a bike that Cagiva, the new owner of the Ducati name, hopes will nullify any doubts that hardcore Duck fans have about the company's ability to carry on the best Ducati sporting tradition. Since Cagiva's acquisition of Ducati in 1984, the only streetbike offered to an anxious American riding public has been the Alazzurra 650—a fine machine but hardly a firestarter of a sportbike worthy of the Ducati legacy.

But now the 750 Paso is here in all its production-line glory, and in appearance alone, it is a knockout. The V-Twin engine and square-tube steel frame are completely enclosed by thick fiberglass bodywork, with overall shapes, lines and proportions that are spot-on. And the entire body is coated in the reddest red paint ever sprayed on a production motorcycle, paint so radiant in the sunlight that it almost hurts your eyes. This is truly the Ferrari of the motorcycle world, and as such is quickly becoming one of the sport's most sought-after status symbols.

Still, the production Paso isn't finished quite as nicely as as the prototype we rode last year. The paint is applied rather unevenly and chips off too easily, and some of the body panels don't fit together quite properly. And many

DUCATI PASO

Finally meeting the lady in red

Under the Paso's smooth exterior is a 748cc motor that can be traced all the way back to the '79 500 Pantah.

of the production bike's numerous aluminum forgings don't have the smooth, polished look of the prototype's. But remember that the hand-built bike we rode at the factory was . . . well, *perfect*. And even if this Paso isn't flawless, it still is just about the most visually striking motorcycle made, a bike guaranteed to elicit more comments per mile than anything else you've ever ridden on—or in.

It's also guaranteed to result in at least one encounter with the law on every ride of any length—as evidenced by the highway patrolman who stopped one of our riders for doing 100 mph on ruler-straight Interstate 5. The officer hadn't clocked him doing 100, hadn't even *seen* him doing 100—and, in fact, the rider had not been exceeding the 65-mph limit. But after one look at the Paso, the cop just *knew* the rider had been doing something highly illegal, so he did his duty and issued a stern warning.

Not that the Paso isn't capable of earning a legitimate speeding ticket. It certainly is an able performer, for its 90-degree V-Twin engine is at least as powerful as any twin-cylinder streetbike motor available in the U.S.—including some that have nearly twice the displacement.

Obviously, the Paso can't even hope to compete with today's multi-cylinder sport-racer motors in terms of pure speed and acceleration; but ridden at a pace more suitable for sport-touring than backroad berserking, the Paso is surprisingly fast—and a sheer delight to hear and feel. The throaty rumble of the V-Twin entertains the ears; and although the 90-degree V-spread makes for almost vibration-free running, the gentle throb of the staggered power pulsations has an almost soothing effect on the areas of the body that come in contact with the machine. And because the torque output seems almost not to vary from just above idle to just below redline, the Paso requires very little gearshifting to be ridden at a rapid pace on a curvy road.

The 748cc, sohc motor, which still features the industry's only desmodromic valve actuation, is essentially the same powerplant that began life in the 1979 Ducati 500cc Pantah. It has gone through several stages of evolution since then, first becoming a 600, then a 650, and most

recently seeing service in the 750cc Ducati F1 racebike. The Paso uses the same large valve sizes as the F1, but is detuned through more-restrictive intake and exhaust systems.

Carburetion also is different from the F1's. Instead of using twin Dell'Ortos, the Paso employs an automotive-style, dual-throat Weber. Cagiva chose this carb to help in meeting America's tough emissions requirements; and, unfortunately, this is one area where the production machine is largely unchanged from the prototype, for the carburetion is erratic, just as it was on the bike we rode last year. The mixture seems so weak at or just above idle that the engine sometimes dies at stoplights, and the bike often requires excessive revving and clutch-slipping to pull away from a dead stop.

Even out on the highway, well away from traffic lights, the carburetion causes problems. When the throttle is held at a steady opening during open-road, legal-speed cruising, the leanness gradually causes the bike to slow down. Dialing the throttle open wakes the motor up again, but this trait is quite annoying and makes it almost impossible to hold a steady speed.

Another pre-production glitch that never got ironed out concerns the dry clutch. Last year, we reported that the prototype's clutch felt worn-out and abused, but the clutch on our brand-new production Paso feels much the same. The all-metal clutch tends to engage rather roughly anyway; but when it is subjected to even a little extra slippage when starting off—a tactic often made necessary by the lean carburetion—it squawks and chatters so loudly that it sounds like you're grinding up tomcats in the gearbox. Not the sort of behavior one expects from a high-performance status symbol.

Many of the good points we raved about, though, also survived the transition from pre-production to production. One big area is handling, where the assembly-line Paso is everything we expected it to be. The bike did gain a little weight, partly because the prototype fuel tank was fiberglass and the production tank is steel, and partly because the bike we rode last year didn't have turnsignals

and mirrors.

But even though the Paso is a tad heavy for a sporty Twin, it still sticks to its line through corners as though it were on rails. When you ride this bike, *you're* the one in charge; you pick the line you want, lean as far as you want and go as fast as you want. The bike simply does as it's told.

Credit much of this competence to the Pirelli MP7S radial tires, which stick to the road more tenaciously than chewing gum sticks to your shoes. And Paso riders will quickly come to love the front brake, which is extremely powerful yet very predictable. Conversely, the rear brake is high in effort and low in feedback, but with such a wonderful front brake on the job, we almost didn't care.

If you have any notion of showing up at the local roadraces, though, take our advice: Don't. Cagiva clearly designed the Paso for road riding, not track racing. Aside from the engine's lack of competitive horsepower, the steering isn't quick enough and the riding position isn't aggressive enough for all-out roadracing.

On the bright side, however, the Paso is much more comfortable than most of the new-generation street-racers from Japan—or for that matter, the hardcore sportbikes that traditionally have come from Ducati. Cagiva compromised in all the right areas to come up with a streetable flashbike, one that is more accurately matched up with the big sport-tourers such as Honda's Hurricane 1000 and Yamaha's FJ1200.

In that light, the Paso compares quite favorably, doing everything in its power to pamper its rider on long rides. The suspension—usually a sore spot on Italian bikes—is excellent. The Marzocchi fork has externally adjustable rebound damping and a ride that strikes an admirable compromise between corner-carving and all-around road riding. To our surprise, our test Paso came equipped with a Marzocchi rear shock instead of the Ohlins that was on the pre-production bike, but we have no complaints about its behavior.

We also are unable to fault the Paso's ergonomics, for it seems to fit just about everyone. The bike is scaled for larger riders, which is quite different from what we find with most Japanese sportbikes. Footpeg location is just about right for riders with long legs; and because the bodywork is all-enclosing, there are no sharp fairing edges for that long-legged rider's knees to bang into. And it's hard to imagine a posterior that wouldn't fit the well-shaped seat. So despite the Paso's appearance of being a living-room showpiece, it is, as we said, a bike made for riding.

Nonetheless, it's hard to escape the feeling that the Paso was rushed onto the market before it was completely finished, for there are numerous annoyances that should have been dealt with before the assembly line was fired up. Getting the bike on its centerstand, for example, is a strength test many riders are going to fail. And not only do the round mirrors glued onto the triangular backsides of the turnsignals look like a cheap afterthought, their low-level location (in line with the rider's hips) allows only a narrow, partially obstructed view of the road behind—and virtually no view at all when the Paso is fitted with soft saddlebags for a sport-touring trip. There's also a tripmeter that can't be seen in the dark, a neutral light that can't be seen in the sun, an absence of places on which to hook bungie cords, and the unsettling fact that the front wheel rams the lower edge of the fairing under hard braking.

We also were disappointed that Cagiva was unable to hit its original target price of $5800 for the Paso. But rather than being an oversight on the part of the company, the $6377 list price simply reflects the stability of the Italian lire relative to the ongoing devaluation of the dollar.

But despite our disappointment with the Paso's price and some of its details, we can't honestly say we're disappointed in the bike as a whole. Glitches and all, this is a fun bike to ride—and to be seen riding. And that simply reinforces our feelings that the Paso has the potential to be Italy's pride and joy, a red-white-and-green standout that can easily hold its own against the best the Japanese have to offer.

But it's not there yet, not quite. Maybe another year of simmering is needed before this gourmet dish will be fully cooked. ⊗

CAGIVA/DUCATI PASO

SPECIFICATIONS

GENERAL

List price	$6377
Importer	Cagiva North America
	700 W. 190th St.
	Gardena, CA 90248
Customer service phone	(213) 538-9337
Warranty	12 mo./unlimited mi.

CHASSIS

Weight:	
Tank empty	463 lb.
Tank full	498 lb.
Weight distribution, front/rear, percent:	
Tank empty	48.6/51.4
Tank full	49.4/50.6
Fuel capacity	5.5 gal.
Wheelbase	57.5 in.
Rake/trail	25.0°/4.1 in.
Handlebar width	26.3 in.
Seat height	30.6 in.
Ground clearance	5.6 in.
GVWR	818 lb.
Load capacity (tank full)	320 lb.

ELECTRICAL

Electrical power	300w
Battery	12v, 19ah
Headlight	60/55w halogen

DRIVETRAIN

Engine	liquid-cooled, four-stroke V-Twin
Bore x stroke	88.0 x 61.5mm
Displacement	748cc
Compression ratio	10.0:1
Claimed power	73 bhp @ 7900 rpm
Claimed torque	55 lb.-ft. @ 6350 rpm
Valve train	ohc, two valves per cylinder, desmodromic actuation, shim adjustment
Valve adjustment intervals	1860 mi.
Carburetion	dual-throat Weber 44DCNF107
Air filter	dry paper
Lubrication	wet sump
Oil capacity	3.7 qt.
Starter	electric
Primary drive	helical gear
Clutch	multi-plate, dry
Final drive	chain
Sprocket sizes	15/38

Gear ratios, overall:1	
1st	12.49
2nd	8.56
3rd	6.66
4th	5.37
5th	4.82

SUSPENSION/TIRES/BRAKES

Front suspension:	
Manufacturer	Marzocchi
Tube diameter	42mm
Claimed wheel travel	5.6 in.
Adjustments	air pressure, rebound damping

Rear suspension:	
Manufacturer	Marzocchi
Type	single-shock
Claimed wheel travel	5.4 in.
Adjustments	spring preload, rebound damping

Wheels:	
Front	MT3.75 x 16
Rear	MT5.00 x 16

Tires:	
Front	130/60ZR16 Pirelli MP7S
Rear	160/60ZR16 Pirelli MP7S
Rear tire revs. per mi.	879

Brakes:	
Front	(2) 11.0 in. disc
Rear	10.6 in. disc

PERFORMANCE

ACCELERATION

Time to distance:	
¼ mi.	13.30 sec. @ 99.64 mph

Time to speed, sec.	
0–30 mph	1.7
0–40 mph	2.4
0–50 mph	3.3
0–60 mph	4.4
0–70 mph	5.9
0–80 mph	7.7
0 90 mph	10.1
0 100 mph	13.4

Top gear time to speed, sec.	
40–60 mph	4.8
60–80 mph	5.7

SPEED IN GEARS

Measured top speed	123 mph
Calculated at 9000 rpm redline:	
1st gear	49 mph
2nd	72 mph
3rd	92 mph
4th	114 mph
5th	127 mph
Engine speed at 60 mph	4230 rpm

FUEL MILEAGE

High/low/avg.	55/46/52 mpg
Avg. range inc. reserve	286 mi.

BRAKING DISTANCE

from 30 mph	29 ft
from 60 mph	128 ft

SPEEDOMETER ERROR

30 mph indicated	30 mph
60 mph indicated	58 mph

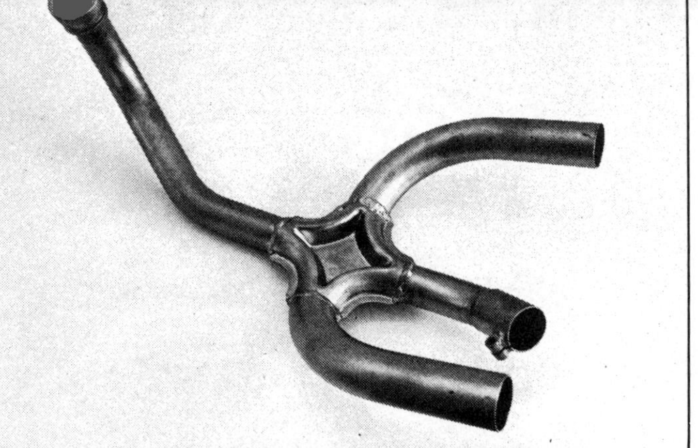

The Tamburini-designed 2-into-2 exhaust system incorporates a unique, diamond-shaped equalizer that diverts half of each cylinder's output into each muffler.

Clean instrument layout includes gauges for fuel level and oil temperature, and a quartz analog clock.

CONTINUED FROM PAGE 29

ride to be a flat-out, take-no-prisoners assault is it necessary to make full use of the entire rpm range and the five-speed gearbox. Agreed, the Paso normally is no VFR or GSX-R beater; but on just the right kind of tight backroad, it'll give either of those 750cc hot-rods all they can handle.

Remember, however, that our impressions were obtained on a prototype motorcycle, so none of this information should be engraved in stone just yet. Not only was the carburetion in the final stages of development, but the bike we rode didn't even have mirrors or turnsignals. We saw a production taillight for the European market that had integrated turnsignals; and Tamburini showed us a prototype fairing that uses knock-off mirrors/turnsignals like those on the BMW K100RS. But yet another taillight, one with more widely spaced turnsignals, will be needed to gain DOT approval in the U.S.; and Ducati had only just begun the arduous process of meeting the EPA's noise and exhaust emissions requirements while we were in Italy.

So at this stage, at least, the Paso still leaves a lot of questions unanswered. But there is no question whatsoever that Massimo Tamburini has pointed the way to a bright new future for Ducati motorcycles. In style and in handling, his wonderful creation is fully competitive with Japanese machinery; in craftsmanship and in quality, it even promises to *exceed* anything the Japanese currently offer. And if Cagiva follows through on its intention to sell the bike in this country for about $5800, the Paso even should be fiercely competitive in the showroom—no small accomplishment for a "production-line Bimota."

All of this is contingent, of course, upon the prototype Paso being faithfully duplicated on the assembly line. But unless Cagiva-Ducati commits a serious blunder somewhere along the way, the Paso is destined to be one of sportbiking's most exciting performers in a long time.

After all, it's Italian. It's red. Most of all, it's *right*. ◙

CAGIVA-DUCATI 750 PASO

SPECIFICATIONS

GENERAL

Importer Cagiva North America
20030 S. Normandie Ave.
Torrance, CA 90502

DRIVETRAIN

Engine	air-cooled, four-stroke V-Twin
Bore x stroke	88.0 x 61.5mm
Displacement	748cc
Compression ratio	10:1
Claimed power	72 bhp @ 7900 rpm
Claimed torque	55 lb.-ft. @ 6350 rpm
Valve train	sohc, two valves per cyl., desmodromic actuation, with shim adj.

Carburetion	Weber 44 DCNF
Lubrication	wet sump
Oil capacity	3.7 qt.
Starter	electric
Primary drive	gear
Clutch	multi-plate, dry
Final drive	chain
Sprocket sizes	15/38

Gear ratios, overall:1

1st	12.49
2nd	8.57
3rd	6.66
4th	5.37
5th	4.82

ELECTRICAL

Electrical power	300w
Battery	12v, 14ah
Headlight	60/55 halogen

CHASSIS

Weight:	
Tank empty	421 lb.(claimed)
Fuel capacity	5.8 gal.(claimed)
Wheelbase	57.2 in.
Rake/trail	25°/4.1 in.
Seat height	31.0 in.

SUSPENSION/TIRES/BRAKES

Front suspension:	
Manufacturer	Marzocchi
Tube diameter	42mm
Wheel travel	5.5 in.
Rear suspension:	
Manufacturer	Ohlins
Type	single shock
Wheel travel	5.4 in.
Wheels:	
Front	MT3.75 x 16
Rear	MT5.00 x 16
Tires:	
Front	130/60-16 ZR Pirelli MP7S
Rear	160/60-16 ZR Pirelli MP7S
Rear tire revs. per mi.	847
Brakes:	
Front	(2) 11.0 in. disc
Rear	10.0 in. disc

PERFORMANCE

ACCELERATION

Time to distance:	
¼ mi.	12.96 sec. @ 102.52 mph*
Time to speed,	
0–30 mph	1.7 sec.*
0–60 mph	4.2 sec.*
0 100 mph	11.9 sec.*

SPEED IN GEARS

Measured top speed 131 mph*

Calculated at 9000 rpm redline:

1st gear	51 mph
2nd gear	74 mph
3rd gear	96 mph
4th gear	119 mph
5th gear	132 mph

Engine speed at
60 mph	4080 rpm

*For reference only. All performance data compiled on prototype motorcycle.

Arai
DUCATI
DESMO
DUCATI

DUCATI 851 EIGHT-VALVE

The birth of a Superbike

HERE'S A HYPOTHETICAL SITUATION FOR YOU: Let's say you were to take a modern Superbike, one capable of qualifying about, oh, eighth for the Daytona 200-miler and running wheel-to-wheel with the likes of Bubba Shobert's Honda and Jimmy Filice's Yamaha, and you entered that bike in Daytona Speedweek's Pro-Twins 50-mile race. And let's say you put a former 500cc world roadracing champion on it. Would that be a fair matchup? Would you expect the bike to have any real competition in the race?

Not likely. But that's exactly what happened last year at Daytona. Marco Lucchinelli, 1981 500cc world roadracing champ, entered the Pro-Twins event on a motorcycle that would have been more at home in the Superbike race. His motorcycle was ineligible for Superbike competition, however, since it wasn't a production machine; but it was perfectly legal for Pro-Twins racing, for one simple reason: It had just *two* cylinders.

That's right—a four-stroke *Twin* capable of running with some of the fastest Fours on Earth. The bike in question: the Ducati 851 Eight-Valve.

As it turned out, a few revitalized relics in the Daytona Pro-Twins event conspired to cover the track with oil; so the race was called off at the halfway point, mercifully reducing the amount of time that Lucchinelli and his obscenely fast works Ducati had in which to humiliate the competition. They won, naturally, going away.

Things have changed since that oil-drenched event last March. In the ensuing months, the Ducati 851 was further developed, refined and raced by the Cagiva-Ducati organization, and has finally been turned into a limited-production reality for sale to the public. Ducati's U.S. distributor, Cagiva North America, plans to bring 50 of the Eight-Valves into the country, strictly for racing, of course. If the American Motorcyclist Association issues the 851 its homologation papers in time, the bike will race again at Daytona—this year, however, in the prestigious Superbike event.

Even at first glance, it is obvious that Superbike racing is precisely what Cagiva has in mind for the 851. Here is a racebike sold exclusively for the track without even a pretense of street duty, yet it has an electric starter, a headlight, a taillight and a keyed ignition switch. The reason for those street amenities is buried somewhere in the AMA's racing rulebook, which stipulates that a Superbike doesn't have to possess such equipment, but must be based on a streetbike that does.

AMA rules also allow twin-cylinder four-strokes to have an edge in displacement, all the way up to 1000cc. This consideration originally was made to allow machines such as big Harley-Davidsons, Moto Guzzi 1000s, and Ducati Milles to have a shot at the winner's circle. But for now, at least, the Ducati Eight-Valve isn't using the full displacement advantage it's entitled to. It already is surprisingly competitive at 851cc.

Obviously, making a Twin run with Fours isn't easy, so

DUCATI 851

the 851 engine is not just an old Ducati motor with some extra cams and valves thrown in; this engine is fundamentally new. It's liquid-cooled, itself a Ducati first, with redesigned centercases that accept a six-speed, close-ratio gearbox. The overhead cams are still belt-driven, but now there are two of them per four-valve cylinder. The included angle between intake and exhaust valves is 40 degrees, much narrower than on previous Ducatis to allow a more-efficient combustion-chamber shape. Thanks to Ducati's desmodromic (mechanically opened *and* closed) valve-actuation system, there are no valve-spring pockets for the ports to be routed around, so the intake tracts run almost dead-straight into the combustion chambers. And the 851 is fuel-injected, eliminating the need for complicated downdraft carburetors.

That fuel-injection system is fairly simple, a Weber-Marelli electronic unit similar to the one Ferrari uses on its Formula One racecars. The computerized system is entirely reprogrammable—that is, if the mixture isn't quite spot-on at any point in the rpm range, it's possible to plug a computer into the system and change its parameters. A nifty concept, even if making those mixture-ratio changes does require someone who is computer-literate and has the software needed to reprogram the system.

Like its engine, the 851's chassis has little in common with past Ducatis—or, for that matter, past Cagivas. Despite common ownership, Ducati and its parent firm, Cagiva, still are quite different companies that haven't entirely integrated as one; each still has separate engineers working on separate projects. The 750 Paso chassis, for example, was a Cagiva project, and the 851 shares practically nothing with it, aside from a footpeg bracket here and a shift linkage there.

But despite being almost entirely a product of the Ducati factory in Bologna, the Eight-Valve also is quite different from Ducati's own recent series of 750cc F1/Montjuich/Laguna Seca production racebikes. The 851's frame is a configuration unto itself, though it bears much similarity to a successful Ducati TT Formula 1 frame built a few years ago by innovative Spanish chassis designer Antonio Cobas. The frame uses a much steeper steering-head angle than do other big Ducati streetbikes, with the exception of the Paso.

The rear suspension is different, as well. Older Ducatis use a series of levers and links to operate a shock located under the fuel tank, but the 851 has a more upright shock that is compressed from both ends—from the top by a large, overhead rocker-arm connected to the swingarm legs via a link rod on each side, and from the bottom by the front of swingarm itself. It's a layout similar to the Full Floater system used on the first Suzuki single-shockers in the early Eighties. Up front, a sturdy Marzocchi M1R fork with externally adjustable rebound damping handles the suspension chores.

In essence, then, the 851 is new from nose to tail. More important, it seems to be reasonably competitive with the best four-cylinder Superbikes in the world—no small accomplishment for a Twin. We're not just taking Lucchinelli's word for it, either; we saw it for ourselves when we track-tested the 851 at Riverside Raceway, spending an entire day flogging this exciting machine through some of the fastest turns in California.

And the first thing we noticed about riding the world's most competitive V-Twin was that the combination of sensations you experience is . . . is all *wrong*. To begin with, you don't expect to start a full-on racebike by touching a button and hearing an electric motor crank the engine to life. Not only that, any European Twin so highly tuned that it can run with Japanese Fours should have the manners of a rabid pit bull. You expect it to sputter and

This racing-only Ducati doesn't have to be civilized, but it is. Even its finish is top-quality.

cough at low rpm, maybe puke a little raw gas out the intake, and suffer from an awful case of megaphonitis, to boot. But the 851 isn't like that at all. Even as it eases through the pits it is impressively civilized, carburating at least as well as any Ducati we've ever ridden, with nary a cough, gag or sputter.

Out on the track, your senses still get mixed inputs as the Eight-Valve winds up to peak rpm, for what you see and feel doesn't jibe with what you hear. Some of your senses are assaulted by relentless, Superbike-fierce acceleration, but the air is filled with the bark and bellow of a big V-Twin rather than the screech and wail of a Four. Besides, the engine doesn't vibrate enough to justify the thunderous, V-Twin hammering that rolls out of the 2-into-2 exhaust system. But the Ducati is dead-smooth, actually shaking and rattling less than most Japanese streetbikes. All wrong.

You learn to ignore those discrepancies quickly enough, but you continue to encounter other inputs that just don't add up. The engine, for example, redlines at 10,000 rpm and continues to pull strongly up until the injection sys-

tem cuts the fuel supply at 10,500 rpm, but it nonetheless pulls impressively hard as low as 5000 or 6000 rpm.

You *don't* learn to ignore that; you learn to use it to your advantage. Not many other racebikes would still let you turn excellent lap times if you lugged the engine 4000 rpm below its power peak. Certainly, most competitive Superbikes wouldn't. And a stock Yamaha FZR750R *definitely* wouldn't.

We know this to be true, for when we went to Riverside to test the 851, we took along an FZR750R for comparison purposes. We didn't have an AMA Superbike laying around, but we did have an FZR in our shop; and we figured that it is about as close to a production Superbike as is available in this country. Since the 851 professes to be just that kind of motorcycle, we felt the FZR would be a perfect match for it.

Wrong again. On the track, the Ducati was superior in nearly every way to the Yamaha. Not only did the 851 walk away from it in roll-on acceleration tests—we expected that much from a V-Twin with a 100cc displacement advantage—but it kicked the Yamaha's fanny in corner-to-corner acceleration and top speed, as well. Every time the two bikes would exit a corner together, the Ducati would stretch out its long legs and flat run away from the FZR. And at the end of Riverside's long back straight, our radar gun caught the Ducati at 152 mph, whereas the Yamaha couldn't top 144.

Both bikes, particularly the Ducati, had a bit more speed in them, but not enough space at Riverside to use it. So, a few days later, we took the 851 out to a long, straight, desolate stretch of road in the desert to find out just how fast it would go. But, alas, 40- to 50-mph crosswinds blew through the area all day, and the Duck managed only 154 mph on its best run, during which it had to bank over into the wind at about a 20-degree angle while going straight ahead. The bike had to be back at Cagiva the very next day for an AMA homologation inspection, so we never had a chance to see how fast it would *really* go. But we feel that

Since the 851's Daytona initiation last year, the appearance of its four-cam engine has changed surprisingly little.

51

DUCATI 851

Ultra-wide Marvic wheels and Michelin slicks (radial in the rear; bias-ply up front) are standard. When you're paying five dollars short of twenty-one grand, you expect all the best components. With the 851, you get them.

Belt-driven double overhead cams, four desmodromic-actuated valves per cylinder, reprogrammable fuel injection and 110 horsepower at the crank; Twins don't get any more advanced than this.

under the right conditions, the 851 could easily nudge the 160-mph mark.

Now, some of you might question our enthusiasm about the Ducati's prodigious power output, seeing as how our FZR is a 750cc streetbike that's legal in 49 states, while the Ducati is an 851cc pure racer that would give an EPA inspector bad dreams for a month. But at Riverside, even the 851's chassis was more than a match for the Yamaha's. The 445-pound Ducati always felt wonderfully light and responsive, almost seeming to change direction at the very thought of turning; yet at speed, it was as stable as a three-story townhouse. By comparison, the Yamaha felt cumbersome and twitchy, even though it is nothing of the sort.

One area where the FZR did have the upper hand was its front fork. The rear-suspension behavior of both bikes was comparable, but the Ducati's Marzocchi fork was consistently harsh around Riverside's bumpy course, often causing the bike to chatter and be imprecise over little ripples at high speed. The Yamaha was able to soak up these same track imperfections much more efficiently.

But in all honesty, that's about the only complaint we can muster. The Ducati is a masterpiece of civility, even though it doesn't have to be. If it vibrated a little, no one would care. If it fell out of the powerband 1500 rpm below redline, no one would be surprised. And if it were a raspy, sputtering collection of bad manners, no one would mind. After all, it is a racing *Twin* that can blow the fairing off any production Four in the 750 class. But there are no catches; the Ducati doesn't force you to tolerate any undesirable behavior.

Well, there is one catch. About $20,995 worth of one. That's how much Cagiva North America wants for an 851. And not only do you have to cough up that kind of money, but Cagiva has to decide if it wants to let you have one. The bikes will be sold though Cagiva dealers, but a potential buyer first has to send a resume with his racing and riding history to Cagiva.

On top of that, although the 851 is the most competitive Twin to hit Superbike racing in a decade, it's not quite capable of *winning* a Superbike main event. Not, at least, as delivered from Cagiva. The engine is in practically the same state of tune as the one in Lucchinelli's 1987 Daytona machine, but that bike would have qualified only seventh or eighth for last year's 200-miler. The 1988 crop of four-cylinder Superbikes will be faster yet, so the 851 has its work cut out for it if it is to be a serious contender for a spot on the victory podium.

On the other hand, there is more potential in the 851 than demonstrated in our test. A thorough race-prep would surely rid the bike of 40 or 50 unwanted pounds as unnecessary items such as the electric starter, the sidestand and the lighting equipment were eighty-sixed and the stock 2-into-2 exhaust system traded for a lighter 2-into-1 like the one Lucchinelli used. That exhaust system would also yield a tad more power, presumably, as would a bit of additional engine hot-rodding and blueprinting. After all that, the 851 might, with a top-rate rider aboard, contest for a Superbike win. But that the bike is competitive at *all* is amazing, a tribute to the talent of its creators—Massimo Bordi, the brilliant young protegé of the famous "father of

Ducati motorcycles," Ing. Fabio Taglioni; and Franco Farnè, Ducati's long-time chief of development.

All things considered, then, that $21,000 ante might seem like a mighty high buy-in. But when you're selling something no one else offers, you usually can name your own price. And right now, there is no other Twin made that can match the 851. Hell, there aren't that many *Fours* that can match it.

So, no, Cagiva isn't planning to sell 851s to everyone. Just to racers who want something they can't get anywhere else—and are willing to pay for it.

SPECIFICATIONS

GENERAL

List price	$20,995
Importer	Cagiva North America
Customer service phone	(213) 538-9337
Engine	liquid-cooled, four-stroke Twin
Bore x stroke	92.0 x 64.0mm
Displacement	851cc
Compression ratio	11:1
Claimed power	110 bhp @ 9600 rpm

Carburetion	fuel injection
Weight:	
Tank empty	417 lb.
Tank full	445 lb.
Fuel capacity	4.6 gal.
Wheelbase	57.1 in.
Seat height	29.9 in.
Tires:	
Front	120/60 V17 Michelin Slick
Rear	180/67 V17 Michelin Radial Slick
Measured top speed	154 mph

Dale Quarterley's Ducati 851

BY STEVE ANDERSON

AYTONA BEACH, MARCH, 1988: IN A FLASH OF RED and white, Stefano Caracchi forces his 851 Ducati 8-Valve under Roger Marshall's powder-blue Cosworth in Turn Two. As the two bikes near collision, the Cosworth bobbles and gives way. The Ducati darts ahead, a lead it will hold through the twisty Daytona infield, then lose on the banking. Last lap, and the entire race comes down to the back-straight chicane: If Caracchi can exit there right on Marshall's tail, perhaps he can use the draft to slingshot past just before the start-finish line. Instead, Caracchi twists the throttle too hard, slides, recovers. That mistake gives Marshall needed feet, and the Daytona Pro-Twins victory. Long seconds later, Dale Quarterley finishes sixth on an older, air-cooled Ducati.

* * *

Sears Point, September, 1988: The same red-and-white 851 is leading another Pro-Twins race. A few feet behind is Doug Brauneck on Dr. John's Moto Guzzi, the fastest of its kind and 1987 Pro-Twins champion. Brauneck is visibly struggling to keep up with the Ducati, and although he manages occasionally to pull close enough to flash a wheel, the rider of the Ducati, Dale Quarterley, clearly has his measure. Quarterley and the Ducati go on to win the Sears Point race and convincingly demonstrate that they deserve what they've already achieved: the 1989 Pro-Twins Number One plate.

* * *

The path connecting the Daytona and Sears Point Pro-Twins races was a long one, with more than a few twists. It began, in part, with Stefano Caracchi, the man who first brought the 851 to America. Caracchi is a good Italian roadracer whose father just happens to run NCR, the tuning company that is to Ducati what Yoshimura is to Suzuki. So, when Carraci's 8-Valve was easily the fastest at

We rode the Ferracci 8-Valve at Sears Point and found it faster, better-handling and more refined than the production 851 Ducati we tested this past spring.

Dale Quarterley and Eraldo Ferracci

Dale Quarterley at Laguna Seca

Ducati 851

Daytona, it stirred controversy, since the other $21,000 Ducati 851s delivered during Daytona bike week couldn't match its performance. Indignant rumors abounded: Caracchi's bike was fast due to special parts; it received its speed from a special fuel injection computer; it wasn't fair. Those racers who expected their $21,000 to buy a win, or at least a competitive ride, were upset.

The story continues with Eraldo Ferracci, the Italian-born, American-based proprietor of FBF, the Fast By Ferracci tuning company. The FBF label has become increasingly familiar at American races, gracing bikes competing and winning in everything from Pro-Twins to vintage classes to drag racing. A white-haired man quick to smile, Ferracci perfected his skills in Benelli's racing department in the early and mid-1960s; later he moved to the U.S. to assist with Benelli's import efforts here. When Benelli sales faded in America, Ferracci didn't; he instead stayed to open his successful and growing engine-building business. At Daytona, he tended to a flock of roadracers, and served as Caracchi's sponsor.

The final thread that wrapped this scenario together was Dale Quarterley. A gangly redhead seemingly too tall to be a motorcycle racer, Quarterley is a friendly guy with a droll sense of humor when he's in the pits. But on the track, he's an aggressive pit-bull of a racer, someone who grew up racing underpowered bikes on tight New England tracks, someone who can play bumper-bikes with the best of them. In 1986, Quarterley was enlisted to race a Ducati-engined Bimota DB1, a bike that handled well but was underpowered. And that ultimately led him to Ferracci, and the beginnings of a partnership. Ferracci (or "Ferrach," as Quarterley calls him) worked his magic on the DB1's Ducati engine, and Quarterley immediately went faster. Beyond that, the two liked each other; at the '88 Daytona races, Quarterley's Pro-Twins ride was a Ferracci-tuned-and-sponsored Ducati F1.

But it was in the aftermath of Daytona where things really got interesting. Caracchi had to return to Europe, but his 8-Valve 851, on loan from Ducati, didn't. Perhaps Ferracci and Quarterley would be interested in showing what was possible with such a bike, Ducati suggested, and keeping the factory informed?

An easy yes, but there was one catch: The ROM chip in this particular 851's fuel-injection computer . . . well, it wasn't quite stock. It was calibrated strictly for racing; and whereas the standard 851 fuel-injection system cut off at 10,200 rpm as a safety measure, this particular chip allowed engine speeds up to 11,000 rpm. The rest of Caracchi's bike, though well-prepared, was standard, just like the other 851s at Daytona and just like the 851 we tested in March, 1988. It even wore the standard muffled exhaust system. And the magic chip had to go back to Italy; after all, it *wouldn't* be fair to let Quarterley and Ferracci have something that hadn't been made available to other Ducati customers.

So, when the 851 went back to Ferracci's shop in Willow Grove, Pennsylvania, it had been turned into a stocker. And when it ran on his dyno, the results were disappointing: The trick but heavy 8-Valve didn't have enough edge over Ferracci's lightweight air-cooled Ducati to make it worth running. "I'm not going to take a bike to the races that can't win," he said. For Road Atlanta, the 8-

The Fast By Ferracci company has become the U.S. clearinghouse for 8-Valve Ducati information, and can supply special parts such as modified fuel-injection chips to serious Ducati racers. Located in Willow Grove, PA, FBF can be reached at (215) 657-1276.

Valve stayed in Pennsylvania, and Quarterley rode the older air-cooled Ducati, finishing second and racking up Pro-Twins Series points.

But speaking Italian and being on a first-name basis with Ducati engineers has its advantages: Ferracci kept telling his contacts in Italy that they could have their bike back if they couldn't help him out with some higher-performance parts. After many phone calls, a new fuel-injection ROM chip arrived, along with the factory "lightweight kit"—a fiberglass tank, featherweight body panels and fairing, a smaller alternator, a simpler rear sub-frame. After that, Ferracci went to work removing and reshuffling parts. Out with the electric starter; the heavy battery could move off the tail and alongside the engine. The fuel-injection computer, also in the tail, could move to the fairing's nose.

These changes helped reduce weight from a stock 417 pounds to about 360, and balanced the weight distribution to a more desirable 50/50. And while the factory ROM turned out to be less magic than thought, and no horsepower secret, it provided a wider usable powerband and allowed the rider to run past the stock 10,200 limit when he needed to avoid a shift.

The real power gains would come from Ferracci. A conservative scientist of a tuner, he makes one small change at a time, judges its effect, understands it thoroughly, then either rejects it, or keeps it and tries the next. His modifications to the 8-Valve were subtle: He reshaped the valve seats, opened up the combustion chambers slightly around the intake valves to unshroud them, welded up revised header pipes to smooth the transition from port to pipe, recontoured the crossover junction of the 2-into-1-into-2 exhaust system. The airbox and hoses leading to it were restrictive, so Ferracci installed larger ones, and raised the gas tank to allow more air in.

By this time, Ferracci was on such good terms with Massimo Bordi, chief engineer at Ducati, that he could request custom ROM chips. "If I wanted the injection two-percent leaner at 9000 rpm, I could just call Ducati and they would make me a new chip." Perhaps not as easy as changing jets, but once the injection was dialed-in for a certain engine setup, there was no further need to fiddle; it could automatically correct for differences in altitude or

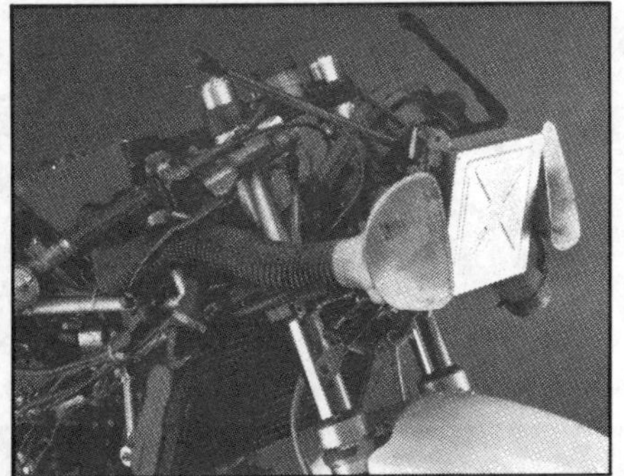

Relocating the fuel injection computer from the tail section to the space normally filled by a headlight helped rebalance the bike for a 50/50 weight distribution.

Any Ducati 8-Valve rivals a submarine for sheer parts density. Clearly no simple Twin, the apparent complexity of the 851 is deceiving; it's not that hard to work on or maintain.

Larger hoses now lead to the airbox; Ferracci found the original smaller ones restrictive. The fuel-injection system is stock except for slight reprogramming of the ROM chip.

An eccentric adjustment in the shock linkage allows changes in ride height, and is a stock 851 feature. Simple rear sub-frame and re-done exhaust junction are unique to the Ferracci bike.

air temperature. Ferracci claims that all these changes added seven or eight horsepower.

In that form, the 8-Valve and Quarterley became a force in Pro-Twins, and dominated the Loudon and Elkhart Lake Nationals. From then on, they were the fastest Pro-Twins entry on the track. They won the Laguna Seca round, though Paul Lewis on the Commonwealth Honda V-Twin spent the entire race trying to pass. At Mid-Ohio, Quarterley had a seven-second lead over Doug Chandler on that same Commonwealth Honda, only to accidentally bump the kill switch. By the time the Ducati restarted, the lead had reversed: Chandler was seven seconds ahead. Quarterley took off after him and was gaining, but the checkered flag ended the race with the 851 still a second behind. But by that point, Quarterley and the Ducati had clinched the championship, and in the series final at Sears Point, beat the Dr. John Guzzi at its best.

After Sears, we had a chance to try Ferracci's 851, and found it an enhanced and polished version of Ducati's production 851. Like the standard bike, it can be ridden from the pits at 2000 rpm, and pulls steadily from 4000.

Like the standard 851, it's way too civilized to be a racebike. The powerband is as flat and smooth as a Kansas wheat field, even if best power can be found between 8200 and 10,200 rpm. There, the intakes resonate and growl, the muffled pipes howl, and the 851 pulls hard indeed, evaporating the short Sears Point straights and hurtling toward the next corner. And the reduction in weight and the improved suspension setup (including a Fox Shock on the rear) have made the racebike handle noticeably better than a stocker.

There is one peculiarity, a raggedness on neutral throttle while cornering; it results from such precise mixture control that the bike responds to the smallest throttle movements. Ferracci says this can be eliminated with a different chip that provides a richer mixture at small throttle openings, but hasn't opted to do so "because it makes the bike lazy." Nevertheless, the Ferracci 851 is an easy-to-ride and exhilarating motorcycle.

But perhaps the most amazing thing about this Ducati is how standard it is. Quarterley and Ferracci receive no financial support from Ducati, and every moment they spend working with the 851 is either a moment away from Ferracci's tuning business, or from Quarterley's many other racing programs (Superbike, AMA/CCS endurance racing, and even stock cars). The purses in Pro-Twins don't do much more than pay some of the expenses. This financial picture, along with Ferracci's conservatism, helps explain why the 851 still wears the stock mufflers: That setup was good enough to win the championship, so why do more yet? For next season, though, more of the horsepower secrets that reside in Marco Lucchinelli's factory Ducati in Europe will make their way to Ferracci's bike; it will almost surely be 10 to 15 horsepower stronger next Daytona.

But don't let that fool you into thinking this a factory effort. The Ferracci/Quarterley team is strictly privateer, fueled far more by passion than by money. Their attitudes are best exemplified by what Ferracci got from Ducati at the end of the 1988 season: a bill. Indeed, after winning the Pro-Twins championship for Ducati, Ferracci was asked to either buy the 851, or return it.

Within a matter of hours, his check was winging its way to Italy. ◙

DUCATIS ARE SUPPOSED TO BE quirky, aren't they? Aren't they weird, as heavy-steering as trucks and as highly strung as opera singers? If that's what you think, it's time for an attitude adjustment, and the bike you see here may be just the tool with which to make that change.

Meet the Ducati 750 Sport, a Duck of a different color. What once may have been quirks have been molded into character, creating a mainstream motorcycle with a difference, a gorgeous piece capable of motoring along with personality and *brio*, which beyond anything else, are the prime elements of the Ducati legend.

Ducati's traditional greyhound sleekness is a part of that legend, and the 750 Sport does not forsake its heritage. Nor does it go against the grain of another Ducati trait: that of going against the grain. The Sport's highly visible tubular frame and its V-Twin engine mark it as definitely different when compared to Japanese sportbikes.

Instead of using an alloy perimeter frame as on most modern sportbikes, the 750 Sport turns to a page from the past: It has the same chrome-moly-tube, triangulated space-frame as used by the F1 production racer of 1985-1987, and by 1988's F1S streetbike. There's a nice piece of traditional continuity here, for those who care about such things. One of the machines that made this method of frame construction famous also was Italian—the Maserati Tipo 60-61 of the early 1960s, called the "Birdcage Maserati" because the frame's wealth of tubes made it look as though it ought to contain something wearing wings and feathers.

The frame uses the bike's 748cc V-Twin engine as a stressed member, feeding loads into it through lugs cast into each side of the engine cases deep in the vee between the cylinders and behind the rear cylinder. But that isn't all. The bike's aluminum swingarm bolts not to the frame but to the bottom-rear of the engine cases, which have been made extremely strong by virtue of internal ribbing.

The engine, vastly oversquare with its 88x61.5mm bore and stroke, is very like that which powered the street-going F1S. The major differences are carburetion and exhaust systems that help it meet current U.S. standards, its use of a Marelli digital ignition system instead of a Japanese-built analog system, and its use

1990 DUCATI 750 SPORT

A Duck of a different color

of oil and air to cool its cylinders a là Suzuki's GSX-R/Katana series. This two-valve engine, with its 10:1 compression ratio, belt-driven cams and desmodromic valve actuation, breathes through a dual-throat 44mm Weber carburetor originally designed for automotive use and used previously by Ducati on the Paso 750.

Not lifted from the F1, or from any other Ducati, is the bike's fork, a Marzocchi M1BB which uses 40mm stanchion tubes. This unit, which offers no provision for adjustment except for oil viscosity and level, works at a rake of 28 degrees—a half-degree more than a Suzuki GSX-R750's—and its trail is 4.8 inches.

When it came time to select brakes for the 750 Sport, Ducati's engineers selected Brembos straight from the 750 Paso: dual-piston calipers with 11-inch discs on the front, and a single-piston caliper and a 10.6-inch disc at the rear. The wheels these brakes act upon are 16-inchers, 3.75 inches wide in front, 5 inches wide at the rear, shod with Michelin A59/

Exclusive? You bet. About 400 Ducati 750 Sports will be brought into the U.S. this year.

tion to detail in both form and finish is carried through to the tail section, which contains a complete tool kit and a small amount of storage space. Cagiva's attention to detail is further evidenced by the tie-wraps used to fasten wiring to the frame members—

humped tank is not overly long, and the switches mounted on those bars are easy to use and offer a reassuring feel of precision and quality. Instruments are by Veglia: a speedo on the left and a tach on the right, both with easily readable black numerals and

The Ducati's space-frame is essentially a triangulated bridge between its two wheels, with the engine bearing some of the stresses fed into the frame.

The Sport's foam-encased tach and speedo are nicely visible, but the bike's warning lights, contained in a pod mounted below the tach, are too dim to be seen in the daylight.

M59 radials front/rear.

First impression of this motorcycle involves its extraordinarily high level of finish. The nicely styled fairing, made of fiberglass-reinforced plastic, is fixed to the bike by 11 Allen-head screws and is beautifully smooth, topped with a coat of clear paint that makes the bike's finish look permanently wet. The edges are nicely shaped and finished, and this atten-

red, to match the bike's red frame. There is at least one small lapse in that attention to detail, though: In order to remove the seat to get to the tool kit, one must first remove the passenger-seat cowling using an Allen wrench that is locked inside with the rest of the tool kit.

Swing a leg over the bike, plant your butt, grip the clip-on-style bars, and the feel is GSX-R, but lighter and with better seating. The bike's plastic-bottomed seat is—in shape, foam consistency and overall comfort—one of the best sportbike seats we've experienced.

The reach to the bars over the tall,

white faces. Not readable at all in anything approaching daylight are the idiot lights mounted in a dark-faced panel below the tach. Their glow is far too feeble for them to be of any real use. Nor did an intermittent short in the bike's ignition switch do much for the tarnished image of Italian electrical componentry.

Another factor that detracted from the bike's otherwise thoughtful design and assembly was that the engine oil filler is located *waaay* down behind the fairing. If you expect to add oil, bring a very long funnel. Another detraction is that since the bike has no centerstand, checking the level in the oil-sight glass is a two-man job.

One distinctly European feature which takes some getting used to is that as you stand the bike upright, its spring-loaded sidestand retracts itself. You must remember to toe the thing into place, and hold it there, before you lower the bike into resting position.

But this bike does not encourage rest. Roll open the choke, switch on the ignition, thumb the starter button, roll the throttle just a little, and the V-Twin coughs to life with an absence of vibration but with a feel, through the grips, pegs and seat, of just enough combustion impulse to tell the rider he's on something other than a Universal Four. As far as power delivery, there's not much below 3000 rpm. Torque peak is at 6350 and horsepower peak is at 8500, and this falls off quickly past 8800 rpm. So, the most-usable range is between about 5000 and 8800 rpm. This is mostly flat power, not the peaky sort found in some Fours, though there is a nice surge when the tach needle swings past 7000 rpm.

The fly in this otherwise excellent ointment is that particularly at low rpm, the engine, at least the one powering the *CW* test bike, stumbled

A LEGEND REBORN

More Duck for your buck

CAN YOU SAY "FASTA" SO THAT IT RHYMES WITH pasta? If so, and if you need to go "fasta" than the 750 Sport will carry you, you're ready for Ducati's 900 Supersport.

After the 906 Paso's European launch earlier this year, it seemed only a matter of time before Ducati did the obvious and hung the 906 motor in the 750 Sport chassis. Doing so not only would create a non-Paso stablemate for the 750 Sport, it also would fill the shoes of that mid-1970s classic, the 900SS—the Ducati of all Ducatis, and to those who dream Technicolor Ducati dreams, the greatest sportbike of all time.

But creating the 900 Supersport required more than a mere engine swap. Though it uses the same 92x68mm bore and stroke as the liquid-cooled 906 Paso, the 900 Supersport's 904cc engine is not liquid-cooled. Rather, like the engines that powered the works Cagiva Elefants in the 1988 and 1989 Paris-to-Dakar Rallies, it uses oil-cooled cylinders and air-cooled heads. Producing a claimed 83 horsepower at

8400 rpm, the new engine uses the same camshafts, cylinders and valves as those Paris-Dakar engines, and it uses the Marelli electronic ignition and 9.2:1 compression ratio of the 906 motor.

This engine, which employs wet-sump lubrication, a six-speed transmission and a dry clutch, has been transplanted into the 750 Sport's "birdcage" frame, which receives one modification: The steering head has been strengthened to accommodate the extra power and few additional pounds of the big engine.

The Supersport's power is immediately apparent. It pulls cleanly in top gear from less than 2000 rpm and will rev freely to its 9000-rpm redline, though there's little point in employing max revs. A grin-inspiring combination of torque and horsepower is available between 3500 and 7000 rpm, and use of the six-speed trans keeps the engine on the boil between those points. When the throttle blade is cranked open and the engine's complete potential is tapped, the new 900SS exhibits truly impressive performance, with no evidence of the flat spot that so plagued the 750 Paso, which used the same carburetor. Weighing 55 pounds less than the 906 Paso, the Supersport I rode in Italy accelerated much more smartly than that all-enclosed bike and was quicker off the line than the high-tech 851 Eight-Valve.

The 900SS's front suspension is considerably uprated from that of the less-expensive 750 Sport; indeed, the performance of its 40mm Marzocchi fork would not disgrace the two-wheeled Ferrari image of the 851. Likewise, the plush, controlled ride delivered by the bike's rear suspension is a surprise especially welcome to those used to the farm-cart ride delivered by Ducatis of yore. It seems impossible that a single-shock system devoid of linkage arms between the shock and the bike's stamped aluminum swingarm can give any sort of progressive response. Yet it does.

The Supersport's brakes deliver performance in line with that of the bike's engine and chassis. At the front are dual, 11.8-inch Brembo discs and four-piston calipers, while at the rear is a 9.6-inch disc.

Unlike with its predecessor, the old SS, you don't have to send the 900 Supersport a telegram to get it to turn. The steering is precise and neutral, and in spite of the bike's 57.1-inch wheelbase, 27 degrees of rake and 4.8 inches of trail, it can be hustled around tight mountain hairpins with ease and confidence. More important, the bike wears tires mounted on 17-inch wheels, and those tires are narrower in section than the 16-inchers mounted on the 750 Sport and Paso. This difference makes the bike easier to lean into a corner under braking than 16-inch-equipped Ducatis.

This is a bike aimed at those likely to be tempted by a modern version of one of Ducati's legendary models. The hope at the factory is that in time, the new 900SS will develop a legend every bit as potent as that of the original 900SS, and in doing so, further polish the Ducati image. With a bike this exciting, that just could happen. Expect to see it in the U.S. no sooner than the 1991 model year, and at a price perhaps $1000 higher than that of the 750 Sport.

—Alan Cathcart

briefly when the throttle was opened after being fully closed. This was particularly noticeable in the higher gears because the engine revs through this flat spot very easily in first and second gears.

With the bike's tall first gear, three grand and some clutch slippage—complete with some juddering from the dry, multi-plate clutch assembly—is needed for launch. Shifting up through the gears finds the bike's clutch-lever action very light. Shifting action is equally light and precise, though less-than-firm pressure on the short-throw shifter will reveal a false neutral between third and fourth gears. This is worth noting because for fast sport riding, third and fourth are the gears of choice: Third can be used from about 55 mph through 90; a shift to fourth brings a drop of about 1200 rpm and speeds high enough to put you in jail. Shifting to fifth brings a further 400 rpm reduction, most useful for droning along in a steady-state cruise.

But never mind steady-state cruis-

The spidery substance of the Ducati's framework reveals much to look at, including the swingarm-mounting point at the rear of the engine cases.

ing; bending corners is what this bike is about, and here its heritage as the development of a production racer asserts itself. The slow, heavy steering so characteristic of yesterday's Ducatis is nowhere to be found. In its place is a lightweight quickness which encourages instant direction changes. So effortless is the handling and so willing is the bike to change lines, even after being committed to a corner, that it seems to follow the rider's vision, going precisely where he looks, when he looks there. Smoothness really pays off here, because the bike is light enough that any roughness in steering input or weight shifting upsets the chassis.

The fork is quite firm in its action and displays the stiction typical of Marzocchi units. But the rear suspension, which is adjustable for preload and rebound damping, delivers a taut, comfortable ride and excellent control. The damping knob, at the bottom-left rear of the shock, has positions numbered from one through six, with intermediate marks between those numbers. We found the best combination of ride and handling with the knob set on three; any more was too firm, any less allowed the rear of the bike to move too quickly.

Riding in textbook fashion, with classic, sweeping cornering arcs—instead of on-the-brakes, late-apex, on-the-gas technique useful for other sportbikes—pays off in dividends of snappy speeds that can be sustained for long periods of time. You don't have to shift much, and you don't have to brake much, either, as the engine's relatively light flywheel and high compression knock the edges off your velocity as soon as you roll out of the gas. It's very easy to flow along at an 8/10ths pace on the Ducati, as no dramatics are required to maintain momentum and get strong drives out of corners.

The only caveat to this predictable, neutral handling involves the bike's brakes, which in feel and in action are positive and progressive. But because the Ductati rolls on wide, 16-inch tires, braking into a corner will make the bike reluctant to fall into the lean it must assume, and braking while leaned over will make the bike want to stand up. These forces are not so powerful that they can't be dealt with, but they are present and they must be gotten used to.

The great fun available from the Ducati 750 Sport will be limited in its availability: Cagiva's estimate is that about 400 750 Sports will be brought to the U.S. this model year, and it ought to be easy to find 400 riders sharp enough to appreciate what this bike offers. Sure, it has to be classified as a limited-production piece. And, yes, as the bike ages, could be there'll be the occasional problem finding parts. And, all right, $6700 for a 750 sportbike may be a bit steep. But hey, trust us: Ride one of these and you won't care. The Sport is a Ducati almost devoid of accustomed quirks, yet one that retains the Ducatis charisma. And if that makes it less of a traditional Italian motorcycle, well, so be it, because that also makes the 750 more of a desirable, modern sportbike.

Call it a Ducati for the next decade.

A THINKING MAN'S MOTORCYCLE? THE 750 Sport comes as close as anything I've seen in a while. It makes few real requirements of its rider, except that he be past the puerile seductiveness of raw horsepower, that he realize he's exempt from the pressure to ride what everyone else is riding.

The Sport doesn't have the top speeds or the hyper-horsepower hit of most other sport-bikes. It also doesn't have their weight, and it doesn't have the feeling—standard equipment with some sportbikes—that it's been sanitized, by virtue of corporate-committee design, of character. This is a bike that grows on you like the subtle charms of a woman who has experienced life. It is the sort of motorcycle you want to reward yourself with for having survived to maturity. That doesn't mean it's a codger's bike; it's far too fast for that. Rather, it means that everything else you've ridden has been training to enable you to appreciate this Ducati.
—*Jon F. Thompson, Feature Editor*

SLEEK AND EXOTIC IN APPEARANCE, and powered by timeless, 90-degree V-Twin engines with exhaust notes that send shivers down my back, Ducatis have always held my interest.

But, as attractive as Ducatis have been, I've always been disappointed after riding them. Not with engine performance, for some of the Ducatis I've ridden produced gobs of power. No, the disappointments resulted from harsh suspensions and balky controls that required arms like Hulk Hogan's to operate.

Even so, I was anxious to ride the 750 Sport. Any motorcycle that looks as good as this one deserves a try. And this time, I wasn't disappointed.

The Ducati 750 Sport is a friendly, refined motorcycle. Its controls move smoothly with little effort, and its Marzocchi suspension, while still a half-step behind state-of-the-art systems, delivers a comfortable ride.

With its newfound livability, this excellent-handling Italian beauty could persuade a lot of people—me included—to become more than just interested.
—*Ron Griewe, Senior Editor*

I LOVE TO LOOK AT THIS MOTORCYCLE. I enjoy looking at details like the tiny frame rails, which seem too delicate to hold the bright-red bodywork in place, let alone harness the power of the engine. And just the fact that you can actually see the engine places this sportbike apart from most of its competition. I like that.

But, and there's always a "but," I don't get anywhere near the same satisfaction from riding the Ducati as I get from simply gazing at it. The fuel tank is wide and square at the rear, splaying my legs, and the throttle vibrates my hand to sleep. That's far from outright damnation, but I expected so much more from the bike. Oh, it does everything I want it to, and it's a remarkable machine, one that most owners will grow to love. But for some reason, I came away with a lukewarm feeling for the bike, untouched, I guess, by the Ducati mystique.

If all I wanted out of a bike were visual thrills, the Ducati would be mine in a minute, but, for now, it's not for me.
—*Camron E. Bussard, Executive Editor*

DUCATI 750 SPORT

SPECIFICATIONS

GENERAL

List price	$6700
Importer	Cagiva North America 5 Washington Ave. Fairfield, NJ 07006
Customer service phone	201/882-9141
Warranty	12 mo./unlimited mi.

ENGINE & DRIVETRAIN

Engine	air- and oil-cooled, four-stroke V-Twin
Bore x stroke	88.0 x 61.5mm
Displacement	748cc
Compression ratio	10.0:1
Claimed power	72 bhp @ 8500 rpm
Claimed torque	53 lb.-ft. @ 6350 rpm
Valve train	ohc, two valves per cylinder, desmodromic actuation, shim adjustment
Valve adjustment intervals	1850 mi.
Carburetion	44mm Weber
Oil capacity	3.4 qt.
Electrical power	300w
Battery	12v, 16ah

CHASSIS

Weight:	
Tank empty	415 lb.
Tank full	438 lb.
Fuel capacity	3.9 gal.
Wheelbase	57.2 in.
Rake/trail	28.0°/4.8 in.
Seat height	31.0 in.
Ground clearance	5.2 in.
GVWR	763 lb.
Load capacity (tank full)	325 lb.

SUSPENSION/TIRES/BRAKES

Front suspension:	
Manufacturer	Marzocchi
Tube diameter	40mm
Claimed wheel travel	5.5 in.
Adjustments	none
Rear suspension:	
Manufacturer	Marzocchi
Type	single shock
Claimed wheel travel	5.3 in.
Adjustments	spring preload, rebound damping
Tires:	
Front	130/60 VR16 Michelin A59X
Rear	160/60 VR16 Michelin M59X

PERFORMANCE

Time to distance:	
¼ mi.	12.44 sec. @ 107.27 mph
Time to speed, sec.	
0-30 mph	1.6
0-60 mph	4.1
0-90 mph	8.7
0-100 mph	11.20
Top gear time to speed, sec.	
40-60 mph	3.5
60-80 mph	4.1
Measured top speed	127 mph
Engine speed at 60 mph	4382 rpm

FUEL MILEAGE

High/low/avg.	44/33/40 mpg
Avg. range inc. reserve	156 mi.

BRAKING DISTANCE

from 30 mph	26 ft.
from 60 mph	129 ft.

SPEEDOMETER ERROR

30 mph indicated	29 mph
60 mph indicated	58 mph

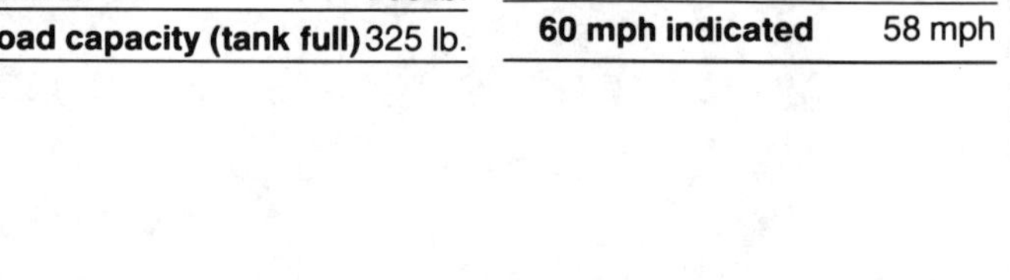

PASO 906

Ducati introduces its engine for the '90s

BY ALAN CATHCART

The Paso 906's revised fairing is based on that of Randy Mamola's GP bike and features ducting designed to enhance the flow of air through the liquid-cooled engine's radiator.

THE 1988 COLOGNE SHOW WAS A LANDMARK FOR THE fortunes of Ducati and for those passionate about the company's motorcycles, but that significance went unnoticed by many show-goers.

Almost everyone assumed the new 906 Paso, introduced at the show, contained just a big-bore version of the venerable Pantah motor, introduced in 1977. You had to scrounge one of Ducati's scarce press kits to realize that all was not as it seemed; that here, in the most understated form conceivable, was the public launch of Ducati's basic power unit for the 1990s—an all-new, two-valve, desmodromic V-Twin with six-speed gearbox and full liquid-cooling.

Designed from the ground up by Massimo Bordi, this engine owes nothing beyond its broad concept to the air-cooled Pantah motor that was the last design of Bordi's illustrious predecessor, Fabio Taglioni. Indeed, there is scarcely a single component from the Pantah that will fit on the 906.

Although some rabid Ducati fans will see the new engine as an admission of defeat, an acknowledgement that the air-cooled engine couldn't be made to live within the hot confines of the Paso's all-enclosing bodywork, the 906 is actually a major element of Cagiva/Ducati's plans for at least the next decade. It is one of a family of three engines, all of which are now in production.

Explained Bordi, "At the lower end of the scale, we have the existing air-cooled Pantah engine, which will continue to be fitted to the entry-level 750 Sport for as long as it remains capable of homologation in a significant number of countries. At the other end, we have the water-cooled 851 Eight-Valve desmo design, which, because of its complication, can only be built in small quantities at relatively high cost. In between, the majority of Ducati motorcycle production will be powered by the new 906 engine and its derivatives."

Those derivatives include versions already under development for street use which employ a mixture of oil- and air-cooling, for use in the dual-purpose Elefant, for example, as well as the fully liquid-cooled design fitted to the 906 Paso, which replaces the 750 model, now no longer in production.

In fact, the 906 Paso has been in production since the beginning of November and is already in the showrooms of Continental dealers, Bordi added. But it may be as late as 1990 before the 906 is sold in the U.S., in part because it needs to be hushed down and cleaned up for American noise and emissions standards.

Bordi began work on the 906 before he began designs for the Eight-Valve engine, whose development was hurried along by the pace of Ducati's involvement in Superbike racing. Thus the Eight-Valve engine appeared before the design it was, strictly speaking, derived from: the 906. The two engines share the same crankcases, six-speed gearbox, dry clutch and high-pressure liquid-cooling system. Apart from the altered stroke of the 906, the engines use the same crankshaft design, though instead of the

PASO 906

851's Austrian-made H-shaped connecting rods, the 906 employs Ducati's traditional ribbed conrod design.

The new two-valve engine's bore and stroke measurements are 92 x 68mm, compared to the 851's 92 x 64mm, giving it a capacity of 904cc. So why call it the 906?

"Do you want the real answer, or the public relations rationale?" asked Bordi. "The real reason is that the 906 logo on the fairing is symmetrical, so I like it better. The official excuse, which I thought up later, is that it's a 900 with a six-speed gearbox."

Running on 9.2:1 compression and unleaded fuel, the 906 engine is a blast from the past fit for the future—like a version of a '60s hit record revamped so completely by one of today's bands that it sounds fresh and new. I can't pretend that my quick ride on one of the first production bikes straight off the factory floor qualified as more than a brief introduction, but in just a few miles I realized what I was riding: a bike powered by the 1990s' version of a 900 Big Twin, the engine that many traditionalists revere as the last real Ducati motor, mainly because of its bevel-drive valve gear.

The 906 has the low-down grunt and smooth torque of the old engine that the higher-revving Pantah never fully enjoyed, but those characteristics are offered in a quieter, less raw-edged package than the engine of five years ago. That may be a drawback in the books of some *ducatisti*, but the fact is that the world has changed, and with ever-more-stringent rules on noise and emissions, and it simply isn't realistic to expect anyone to market a 900SS anymore.

The 906 pulls from practically zero—with strong torque as low as 2000 rpm—up to the nine-grand redline, with claimed horsepower of 74 bhp at the rear wheel (88 bhp at the crank), delivered at 8000 rpm. This ultra-wide powerband, exceptional even by Ducati standards, is due mainly to Bordi's top-end design. It is based on Pantah principles with the same 60-degree valve angle, but with a completely new "triple-hemisphere" combustion chamber design, flat semi-slipper pistons and large inlet and exhaust valves.

Big valves often lead to an engine that doesn't run well down low, but thanks in part to the Marelli digital ignition, the 906 has a remarkably tractable engine. The same twin-choke 44mm Weber carb is fitted to the 906 as on the 750 Paso, but the massive flat-spot embarrassingly and incurably present on most Pasos appears to have been eliminated. The bike I rode was picked at random off the production line, so either there's at least one lucky owner or Ducati really has licked the problem.

With its new engine, the 906 Paso should knock off 12-second quarter-miles, and a prototype has already been clocked at 136 miles an hour. The performance gains come in spite of the inevitable weight penalty of the bike's liquid-cooled engine. It scales 159 pounds complete with carb, and brings the claimed dry weight of the complete bike to 452 pounds, compared to the air-cooled 750 Paso's claimed 430 pounds.

Comparison of the two versions of the Paso is appropriate because the 906 uses the essentially the same chassis and components as the 750, with some modifications. The most obvious change is the white base to the red body-

Hidden behind cam drives and a maze of plumbing is the heart of the Paso 906, complete with a set of token fins that give the engine an air-cooled look.

Triple-hemisphere combustion chambers, flat-topped pistons and oversized valves give the 906 engine the power that helps make it a successor to the 900SS.

work, which has the effect of lightening the bike's previous, rather-bulbous appearance. There are also some revisions to the fairing, which now incorporates ducting both in the sides and internally to achieve maximum flow of cool air into the radiator and hot air away from it, and is based on the bodywork designed by Massimo Tamburini for Randy Mamola's 500cc GP Cagiva.

The only major change to the 906's chassis from that of the 750 is its front suspension. The same 42mm Marzocchi fork is used, but its travel has been reduced slightly, presumably to curtail the front fender from contacting the bodywork during full-on stops, a problem that plagued some 750 Pasos. Additionally, the steering-head angle has been kicked out a degree to 25 and the trail also increased, all to offer more-stable handling.

Certainly the 906 seems to handle in a more relaxed and predictable way, especially under braking, than the 750 Paso. But the 906, like the 750, is equipped with 16-inch wheels and still sits up on you if you try braking when it's cranked over, if a bit less than before. Bordi recognizes the problem and claims that until 17-inch wheels can be fitted to the 906, new-generation Pirelli radials, expected shortly, which have a different, less rounded profile than the present design, will resolve the problem. I hope so, especially as the trait spoils enjoyment of what is otherwise light and confident steering.

While Bordi's at it, I hope he increases the size of the front discs and replaces the ancient twin-piston Brembo calipers. These items work well in average use, but from experience with them on the 851, I don't think they'll be powerful enough at the sort of speeds owners of the heavier 906 are likely to attain.

Though the Paso doesn't excite me in the way that the elemental 750 Sport does, I must admit Bordi has succeeded in producing an engine that meets all the requirements of the 1990s in an engineering sense, while still retaining the lusty nature and lilting, offbeat grunt of a traditional Ducati V-Twin. Because of that engine, the 906 is a rider's delight, likely to become as much of a classic in its own time as the 900SS and the Pantah were in theirs, yet accessible and acceptable to a far wider range of customers than the trick, expensive 851 Eight-Valve.

So, rather than being an admission of defeat, the 906 is instead a declaration for the future. And it's right the first time: Half a decade after the last bevel-drive Ducati was made, the Big Twin is back.

Italian Alternative
DUCATI 851 SPORT

FOR MANY PEOPLE, ANY TALK about sportbikes is actually a conversation about Ducatis. Reverential whispers about 750 and 900 Supersports could lead you to believe the genesis of today's modern sportbike was in Italy. Of course, there is more than a grain of truth to that, and, at the very least, the bright-red, 1990 Ducati 851 Sport seen here is proof the Italians still know a thing or two about building outstanding sportbikes.

As evidenced by our 500 miles on the bike and by the qualifying times at Daytona this year (a race-kitted 851 was third-quickest, running against similarly modified 750cc Fours), Ducati offers a sportbike with every bit the refinement, power and handling of its four-cylinder Japanese competition.

Originally, we had planned to include the 851 in this month's 750 sportbike comparison. Unfortunately, that didn't happen due to logistical problems. We had requested a test unit from Cagiva North America months earlier, but despite our best efforts to get the bike, and the company's assurances that it was on its way, the 851 did not arrive until after we had completed the comparison test. Still, we have a good idea where it fits in the class.

Our 851 went 150 miles an hour; two miles per hour faster than the Suzuki GSX-R750. We tested one of the very first 851s brought into America back in 1988, and that machine went 154 miles an hour, but the new bike is more refined and consid-

erably quieter than that early bike. Our new 851 sprinted through the quarter-mile with a time of 11.26 seconds, just a fraction behind the Yamaha OWO1's 11.20-second time, which was the third-quickest of the

750s. So, performance-wise, the 851 is in the hunt with the other bikes.

That an eight-valve Twin, albeit one with liquid-cooling, desmodromic valve actuation and 100cc of extra displacement, could even get close to the inline-Fours of the ZX-7, GSX-R and OWO1, and the V-Four of the RC30, is quite an achievement. Part of the explanation can be traced to the Weber fuel-injection system employed on the 851. The electronically controlled system meters fuel into the cylinders, compensating for ambient air temperature, altitude, throttle opening and engine speed. The result is nearly perfect running, without any flat spots. We did experience some occasional cold-starting problems, however, as the engine was reluctant to get going on chilly mornings, and it would backfire on trailing throttle. >

DUCATI 851

Once warmed up, though, the engine performed wonderfully. With more low-end grunt than the RC30, the 851 chugs through the corners, then blasts out of them with a powerful lunge accompanied by a deep-throated exhaust note. It pulls strongly up to about 9000 rpm before the power begins to drop off just before the 10,000-rpm redline. The engine is as easy to use as the RC30's, though it lacks the Honda's mid-range power and top-end rush.

It also lacks the smooth-shifting RC gearbox. The six-speed transmission on the Ducati works great at higher engine speeds, but gets a little balky with low-rpm, or timid shifts. Perhaps with more miles, the transmission will loosen up. One thing missing is the dry clutch that is standard on the European models.

Mated to the stout engine is a chassis as beautiful as it is functional. A series of triangulated sections made out of chrome-moly steel tubes tie the steering head to the aluminum, box-sectioned swingarm. A 42mm Marzocchi fork with well-matched damping and spring rates is mounted up front, and a Marzocchi shock takes care of rear-suspension chores.

Between the stiffness of its frame and the precision of its suspension units, the Ducati handles on par with the rest of the class on the street—it would have been interesting to run the 851 against the 750 Fours around Riverside Raceway. It feels lighter than all but the RC30, although at 474 pounds it's actually heavier than all but the ZX-7. The fork is a little on the firm side, and initially, the shock was set way too stiff, jarring the rider over bumps. We set the rebound damping between the third and fourth clicks and the compression damping on its third setting, and that helped considerably.

For the most part, the Ducati falls right into the middle of the hardcore 750s in terms of performance, handling and price. It sells for $10,900, and so far, only 130 of them have been brought into America. It's quite a bit more expensive than the Suzuki or Kawasaki; but it's a far less expensive limited-production motorcycle than the RC30 or OWO1.

Regardless of the price, the Ducati is unique among the class. It has a distinctive look, sound and feel, and it forces you into no more compromises than the other bikes. But above

Large –50mm– throttle bores direct the air/fuel mixture into the cylinder heads. A computer tucked beneath the seat determines the correct mixture.

and beyond being a great motorcycle, the 851 gives you something the RC, OW, ZX and GSX-R can't: A connection with some of the most-legendary sportbikes ever made. ◙

Ducati goes its own way, and continues to make its frames out of lightweight chrome-moly tubes while the Japanese insist on aluminum—beam-type frames for their serious sportbikes. The 851 rides on 17-inch wheels front and rear.

SPECIFICATIONS

GENERAL

List price	$10,900
Weight:	
Tank empty	474 lb.
Tank full	506 lb.

PERFORMANCE

Time to distance:	
¼ mi.	11.26 sec. @ 121.29 mph

Time to speed, sec.	
0-30 mph	1.3
0-60 mph	3.2
0-90 mph	6.3
0-100 mph	7.7

Top gear time to speed, sec.	
40-60 mph	4.1
60-80 mph	4.3
Measured top speed	150 mph

BRAKING DISTANCE

from 30 mph	25 ft.
from 60 mph	124 ft.

DUCATI

A NEW PASO, A BETTER 851 AND THE RETURN OF A GRAND OLD NAME

DUCATIS AS RAW-EDGED street racers that are high on charisma but low on everyday practicality?

Naw. Well, yeah, maybe. In fact, the all-enclosed Paso 750 was launched in 1986 with the express mission of countering that notion. Conceived as a softer, quieter, more

A renewed Paso. This is the 907 ie, Ducati's great red hope for sportbike riders looking for something a little different.

user-friendly motorcycle which might lure customers away from Japanese brands, the Paso's styling understated the unique appeal of the Italian V-Twin engine it clothed. Hailed for its stylish, non-threatening image, the Paso did the job it was supposed to do. It made desmodromic converts out of customers who might otherwise have confined their shopping list to four-cylinder Japanese bikes. For a while, the Paso was chic.

But not for long. Because in an effort to lighten throttle-cable pull and make the bike less of a chore to ride, Massimo Bordi, the chief Ducati engineer, fitted the Paso with a car-type, two-barrel Weber carburetor, and this, with its horrific flat spot, turned out to be the Paso's Achilles heel. Ducati struggled to solve the

problem, but never really succeeded. And idiosyncratic handling resulting from the use of 16-inch wheels—this at a time when other manufacturers were rejecting them—was another factor in the Paso's less-than-anticipated sales numbers.

Replacement two years ago of the 750 engine with a liquid-cooled, two-valve, 904cc desmo motor using the same bottom end as the 851 Superbike resulted in the 906 Paso. But this met with limited success, since it was still endowed with many of the faults of its smaller-engined predecessor, especially the Weber carburetor.

But that was then. For 1991, the Paso has been updated again, and this time the Italians have got it right. Think of the new 907 ie as a Paso that's been sent to finishing school.

The two letters following the 907 designation provide a clue to what may the most significant change incorporated in this new Paso. They stand for "iniezione elettronica."

That's right, Bordi has hung Weber/Marelli electronic fuel injection (EFI) onto the 906 Paso's engine. Why not fit twin Mikuni carbs as on the new 900SS? Because the 907 ie is aimed straight at the American market, and EFI is needed to meet emissions regulations here. Indeed, the first batch of 200 bikes built were destined not for Japan, usually the recipient of the first supplies of each new Ducati model, but the U.S., where the 907 Paso will be homologated and put on sale as soon as possible.

Apart from the installation of EFI, the 907 engine is essentially as fitted to its 906 predecessor. But the rest of the bike has been completely revamped, with the same 17-inch Brembo wheels fitted front and rear as on the 851 sportbike, these shod with Michelin radials. Though the unlovely looking square-tube chassis remains basically unchanged, the steering geometry has been altered to accommodate the 17-inch hoops, and to offer more stable handling. The old-style Brembo brake system previously fitted has been junked, replaced with more modern components in the form of twin Brembo 12.6-inch floating discs and the latest-spec four-piston calipers. At the rear, the alloy swingarm is now the same as fitted to the 851, with racing-type adjusters rather than cam-type ones, while all the odds and ends like footrest hangers, controls and instruments have largely been retained from the previous model.

The rather bulbous Paso bodywork

The Leader of the Quack. The 851 Sport is updated for '91 with an upside-down fork, Öhlins shock and an improved fuel-injection system. As last year, supplies of the 1991 Super Duck will be limited.

Until the late '70s, the old Ducati 900SS was considered the world's best handler. The new 900 Super Sport, the blending of 851-type running gear with an air-cooled, two-valve desmo engine, hopes to tap into that reputation.

has been subtly restyled to incorporate narrower, more streamlined contours, which gives the bike a lighter look, and the color scheme is now red all over. That red is a darker hue than featured on the 906 Paso. This happens to be the same exact shade of red as employed by Ducati on its 851s in road and race form, and by a certain car manufacturer at nearby Maranello for its products.

Perhaps the most obvious change to the Paso 907's styling is the replacement of the controversial but distinctive "blind" windscreen by a stylized version of a NACA duct. It was Virginio Ferrari, former GP racer and TT F1 world champion, and

It-ain't-pretty-but-it-works Dept.: Under that square-section steel frame, very similar to that of the original Paso, lurks a 90-degree V-Twin equipped with desmo valves. This one also boasts electronic fuel injection.

most recently manager of the now-defunct Cagiva 500cc GP team, who first modified the screen of his personal Paso roadbike a couple of years ago in this way. The idea was to deflect the airflow over his head at speed, rather than at his helmet visor. Cagiva/Ducati's head of design, Massimo Tamburini, saw the modification and adopted it on the 907 after tests proved that it worked.

Offered the chance to spend an afternoon in the company of one of the first batch of 907s destined for the U.S., I found, first of all, that the two-valve engine has been transformed by the EFI, and has not a trace of the Weber-derived flat spot. It'll run as low as 2500 rpm in top without snatching as you pull away, which is just as well, because the light-action dry clutch is rather hard to slip. Without a hiccup in the power delivery up to a near-five-digit redline, and with extra torque provided by softer valve timing and longer stroke compared to the more powerful EFI-equipped 851, there has to be a real question mark as to the need for the 907's six-speed gearbox. Such a flexible and torquey engine as this could perfectly well be fitted with a five-speed cluster.

The riding position is more comfortable than before, because you don't end up sliding down the seat to crush precious bodily parts against the tank as was the case with previous Pasos. The bars are quite short, so the rider's hands end up close together in what seems like a Latin version of a BMW Boxer riding stance. The screen duct really works, with the little lip deflecting the airflow upwards so that there's not so much turbulence around your head as before. But it's in the hills that the modifications to the Paso chassis come into their own. Getting rid of the 16-inch wheels is the biggest improvement, and as a result of that change, the Paso 907 ie is much more stable and predictable, especially when braking deep into a turn. The revised bike has become the easy-handling, rider-friendly bike the Paso was always supposed to be.

That's not to say that the sporting flair endemic in a Ducati has been ironed out: far from it, since the wide wheels, Michelin radials and potent brakes coupled with really well-balanced steering encourage loads of confidence. Whereas before it was possible to scrape the sides of the bulkier, old-style Paso fairing because of the low ride height of the 16-inch wheels, the slimmer bodywork and larger-diameter wheels of the ie give more than adequate ground clearance even in a dedicated onslaught on a mountain pass. The latest-type Marzocchi M1R fork is fitted, which worked well enough over the smooth surfaces I encountered on my ride, though with the stopping

Serious competition for Honda's VFR750? Maybe. Depends on the price, which, at presstime, had not been announced.

power of the brakes now fitted, it would have been nice to see the uprated level of equipment on the bike maintained by fitting Marzocchi's new upside-down fork.

My short ride on the 907 left me wishing I'd had more time, which is not a reaction I've had to any Paso, a bike which always struck me as being a shameful waste of a perfectly good Ducati engine. The fuel injection and the chassis modifications have resulted in a bike which is a serious contender for the sort of marketplace slot currently occupied by Honda's superb VFR750F.

Bordi and his development team have transformed a stylish but flawed machine into a terrific motorcycle. It's taken longer than it should have, but the Ducati Paso now is thoroughly sorted out.   —*Alan Cathcart*

MORE SPEED FOR THE SPORT

How to doctor a Ducati 750

THERE MAY BE, SOMEWHERE, A motorcycle that wouldn't benefit from improved throttle response, better brake-lever feel and improved suspension compliance, but the Ducati 750 Sport isn't it.

Don't get us wrong. The Sport is a terrific machine, full of fun, crammed with character, and when we road-tested it in our December, 1989, issue, we found much about the bike that was worthy of praise. We also found a few things we didn't much care for. Leading the complaint list was a throttle-response glitch in the form of a cough, a buck, a hesitation, when the throttle blades in the bike's automobile-derived Weber two-barrel carburetor were abruptly cranked open. This was most noticeable when the throttles were opened at mid to low rpm after the engine had been on trailing throttle. Getting the most from a bike as light and responsive as the 750 Sport requires absolute smoothness, and this throttle glitch stands smack in the way of achieving such smoothness. Additionally, no motorcycle has any business going out a factory door with such an annoying problem. And a premium 750, with a $6700 list price, certainly doesn't.

So we fixed it. And while we were at it, we fixed the bike's vague front brake feel and its stiff and uncompliant Marzocchi fork. We also buffed the hard edge off its uncompromising and uncomfortable sportriding position, we reduced its tendency to stand up in a corner when the brakes were clapped on, and, for good measure, made a few other detail changes.

First, the carburetion. We hauled the bike to Pro Italia Motors (3518 N. Verdugo Rd., Glendale, CA 91208; 818/249-5707), the local Ducati outlet, and said, "Please fix it!" Bob Weindorf, the Pro Italia Duck doctor, responded by pitching the Weber and the bike's stock 2-into-2 exhaust system. Weindorf replaced the Weber with a pair of Dell 'Orto 36mm carbs. Into these he put #135 main jets, #60 pilot jets, K5 needles, 60/4 slides and light throttle springs. Necessary for this was a Malossi carb kit, which includes carbs, manifolds, cables and air cleaners. These last items were tossed in favor of K&N filters.

To handle the exhaust, a Verlicchi 2-into-1 header and reverse-megaphone "muffler" were installed. The result was absolutely, er, stunning. Most noticeably, the Duck now has a harsh, raspy bark rather like a lightly muffled Chevy small-block V-Eight. And it runs absolutely cleanly, carbureting almost as though it was fuel-injected, with a much stronger midrange than stock, and absolutely no trace of throttle-response problems. We tried several other mufflers in

Lung transplant: To enhance the Duck's breathing, a pair of Dell 'Orto carburetors was installed in place of its stock Weber. Vive la différence!

search of a more moderate exhaust note, but while most delivered mellow sounds, the bike ran noticeably better wearing the reverse-mega. Just have to short-shift around town, and hope the *gendarmes* have soft spots for Italian motorcycles.

As a result of this small amount of work, the bike's quarter-mile time went from 12.44 seconds at 107.27 mph to 12.06 seconds at 111.66 mph. And its roll-on time from 60 to

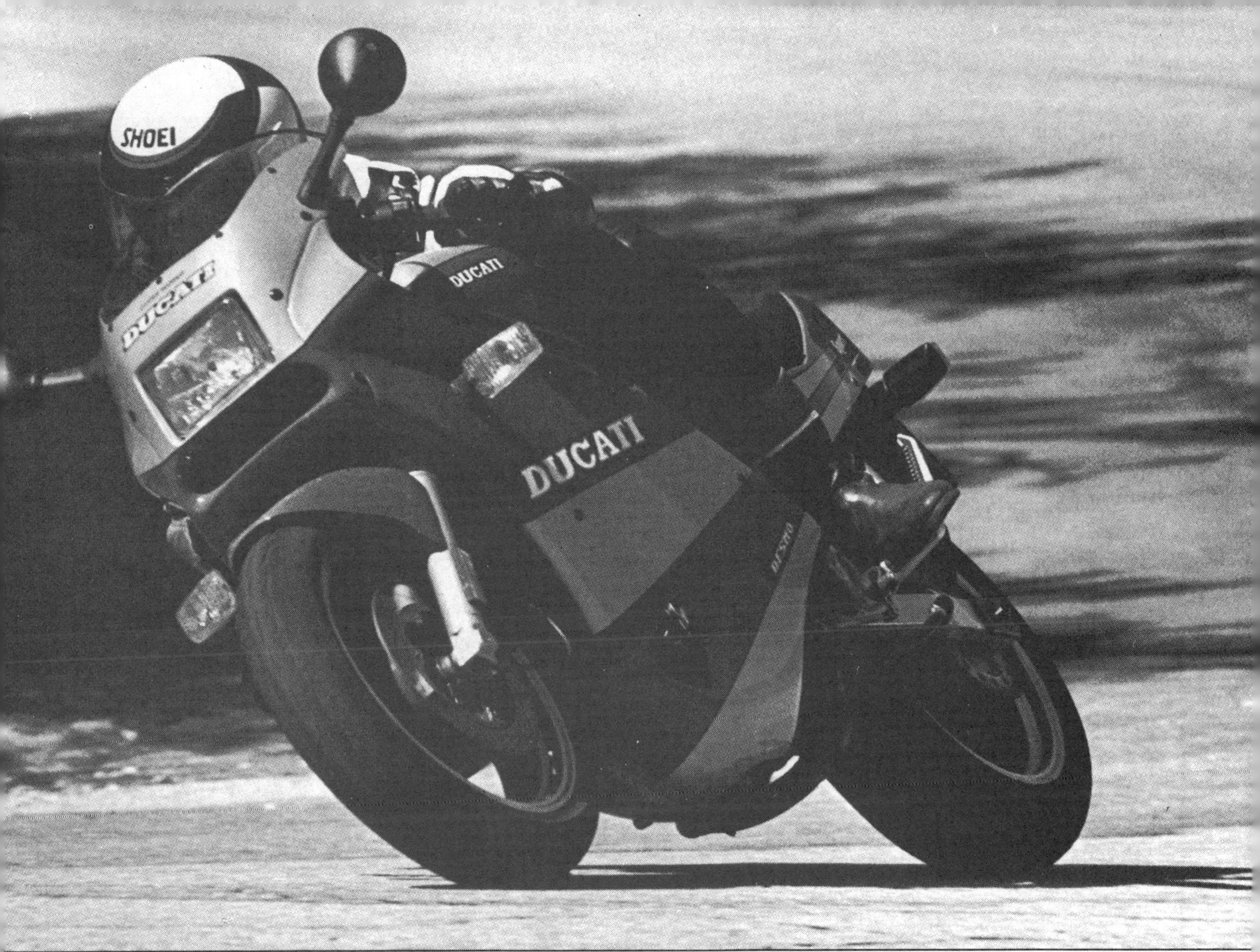

HOTO BY JON F. THOMPSON

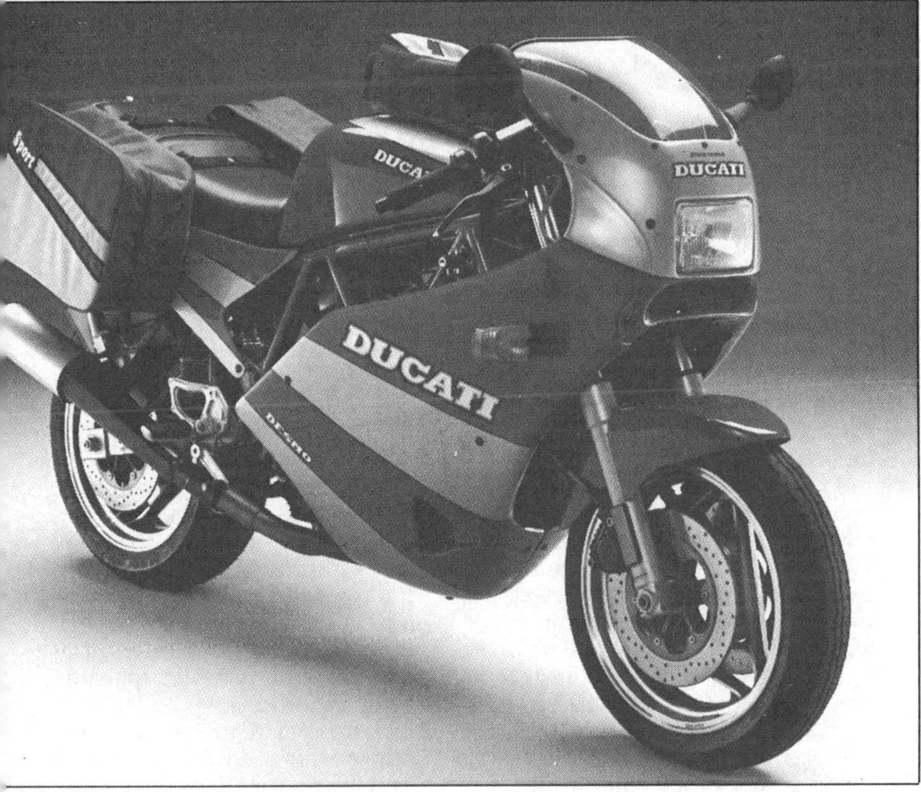

Installation of the tailor-made RK soft luggage transformed the bike into an extremely competent, if somewhat hard-edged, sport-tourer.

Pro Italia's ventilated clutch cover helps clutch performance by keeping its dry plates cool, and it adds to the bike's pose quotient by making audible the dry clutch's clatter when it's disengaged. Just like a racebike.

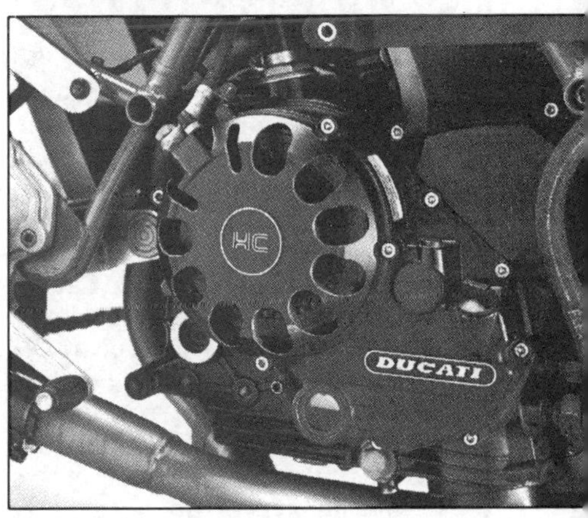

80 mph in top gear went from 4.10 to 3.45 seconds. We'll take it!

That handled, other matters were addressed. Front brakes got greatly improved feel from a set of braided steel lines made up for the bike by Weindorf. Fork oil, 7.5-weight stock, was replaced with 5-weight Bel-Ray, a change which delivers slightly less rebound damping than we like during very hard cornering, but which, the rest of the time, provides a huge improvement in the compliance of this bike's rather basic fork.

We played around a bit with tires, not completely happy with the tendency of the bike, on its as-delivered 16-inch Michelin radials, to stand up in corners when the brakes were applied. A set of Metzeler Comp Ks greatly reduced this tendency and enhanced the bike's overall stability, but at the expense of slower, heavier steering and a harsher ride. A set of Pirelli radials proved a terrific compromise.

Riding position was improved through a set of Pro Italia handlebars an inch higher than standard. And

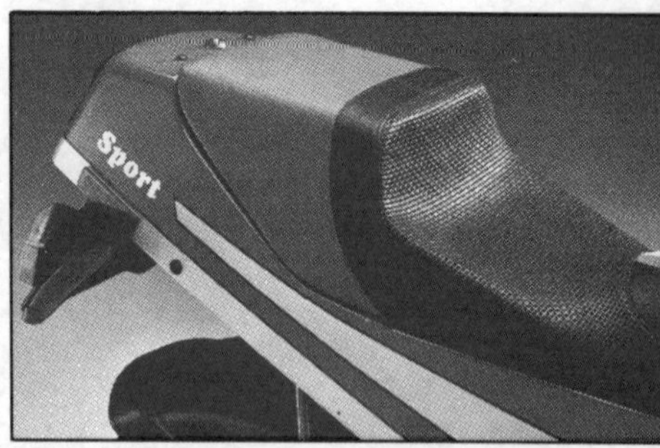

The custom Corbin seat applied to the Duck wasn't as comfortable as the stock unit, but was easier to move around on. Stubby rear turnsignals from a 750 F1 cleaned up the bike's rear profile.

The 90-percent Solution

A simple piece of tuning and a pair of fresh mufflers almost solve a problem. But not quite.

CURING THE DUCATI 750 Sport's carburetion woes doesn't have to involve an expensive carb swap. Or thus quoth Eraldo Ferracci, wizard Ducati tuner and master wrench behind the Fast By Ferracci (1641 Easton Road, Willow Grove, PA 19090; 215/657-1276) roadracing stable.

Okay, we said, prove it. So Ferracci shipped us a bone-standard 750 Sport upon which he had laid his considerable expertise. The result is, well, close, very close, but no cigar.

This carburetion flat spot, well-documented since Cagiva first began slapping Weber two-barrel carbs on its Ducati V-Twins, was attacked by Ferracci on two fronts. He reduced the exhaust system's back pressure by installation of a pair of his own silencers. And he slightly enrichened the Weber's primary circuits by changing its standard #55 primary jets to #60 jets and backing the air screws out a turn-and-a-half. That, Ferracci said, was all the bike needed.

We took the bike on a long street ride, and then hauled it to the dragstrip, to find out just how well these changes work. At the dragstrip, they work wonderfully. On the street, they work a bit less well.

At the strip, the uncorked Sport blitzed through the quarter-mile in 12.20 seconds at 109.48 mph. This was not quite two-tenths of a second slower than our project bike equipped with Dell 'Orto carbs, but it was significantly quicker and faster than the 12.44-second, 107.27-mph run of that bike with stock carburetion. And the FBF bike's top-gear 60-80mph roll-on time

A minor carburetor fiddle and different mufflers were all it took to whack two-tenths from the 750 Sport's quarter-mile time. Those changes helped, but did not eliminate, the well-documented problems associated with the bike's stock Weber carburetor.

was identical to that of the Dell 'Orto-carbureted 750 Sport.

On the street, though the FBF mufflers produced a much more mellow and pleasing note than the hard-edged racket made by the Verlicchi system on the Pro Italia bike, the Weber's ill manners were still present, though they occurred much less frequently and in greatly abated form. Additionally, the engine's pick-up, when the throttle was blipped for a downshift, wasn't as clean and as sharp as it should the bike's pose quotient was up-graded with a vented clutch cover, which looks cool, which helps the bike's dry clutch plates stay likewise, and which releases the racy clatter of those plates for all the world to hear. A set of polished alloy brake and clutch reservoir covers, a pair of short-stalk rear turnsignals from an F1 750, a Corbin custom seat and a set of matched soft luggage from RK Accessories completed the package.

None of this has been inexpensive, but the results are worth the cost. The bike works great, sounds great, looks great, and is more fun than a barrel of *gelato*. We just might have to keep it. ⊠

The completed project: Lean and ready to roll.

Ferracci's mufflers tuck in nicely along the Ducati's flank, produce a rich, mellow tone, and flow large volumes of exhaust.

have been. So, as we said, close, very close, but not a 100-percent solution.

There is this, though. The light amount of tuning Ferracci did to this bike significantly up-graded its performance; a gain of more than two-tenths of a sec-ond in the quarter-mile is noth-ing to sniff at, especially when it can be accomplished so easily and inexpensively.

The mufflers, you see, cost $187 each, and the idle jets cost just $3 each, for a total about $700 less than the Pro Italia car-buretor-exhaust transplant. So the changes wrought to this par-ticular Ducati might not have re-sulted in perfection, but they're not too far short of that ideal.

—Jon F. Thompson

Mounting up the chunky Metzeler tires meant dealing with minimal front-fender clearance, and installation of a rear sprocket spacer and an alternate countershaft sprocket to move the drive chain away from the fat rear rubber. The tires gripped wonderfully and reduced the bike's tendency to stand up under breaking, but slowed the steering and made it heavier-feeling.

SUPPLIERS

Malossi carburetor kit
Pro Italia
3518 N. Verdugo Road
Glendale, CA 91208
818/249-5707
Price: $575

Verlicchi exhaust system
Pro Italia
Price: $479

Filters
K&N through Pro Italia
Price: $23

Turnsignal stalks
Pro Italia/Cagiva USA
Cost: $40

Handlebars
Pro Italia
Price: $140

Braided-steel brake lines
Pro Italia
Price: $140

Vented clutch cover
Pro Italia
Price: $99

Installation labor
Pro Italia, shop rate $40/hour
Price: $270

Seat
Corbin Saddles
11445 Commercial Parkway
Castroville, CA 95077
800/538-7035
(In Calif. 800/662-6296)
Price: $179

Soft Luggage
RK Accessories
5150 Petrified Forest Road
Calistoga, CA 95492
707/942-0120
Price: $270

CORTEZ'S CONQUERER

Race-testing Fast By Ferracci's $10,500 GP2 Replica

YOU SAY YOU WANT TO BUY a roadracing motorcycle, but you're not interested in a Japanese production bike? Have we got a deal for you.

Cagiva North America has stepped into the racebike-for-sale biz, teaming with Fast By Ferracci to offer replicas of the Ducati 750 Sport on which Fabian Cortez III won the 1990 AMA Pro-Twins GP2 championship. And you don't need to submit a racing resume for approval. Just stop by your local Ducati dealer, plunk down a check for $10,500, hold your breath for four weeks, and presto, you're the proud owner of a Daytona GP2 Replica, so named in honor of Cortez's win at Daytona 1990.

Rarely has racing been this turn-key.

Upon receiving your order, Cagiva North America ships a stock Ducati 750 Sport to Fast By Ferracci, where Eraldo Ferracci and his band of devoted desmo diddlers transform it into something more suitable for racetrack use.

Ferracci begins by removing most of the parts that make the bike street-legal, then replaces the battery with a smaller, lighter unit, retaining the stock charging system. The starter motor is removed and the wiring simplified somewhat, but Ferracci stops short of removing the ignition switch. Like we said, turn-key.

Ferracci is best known as an engine builder, and true to form he has tweaked the 90-degree, four-stroke V-Twin for maximum performance. The engine is first disassembled, then blueprinted and reassembled using Carillo chrome-moly connecting rods and Ferracci's own 12:1 high-compression pistons. NCR #7 cams offer increased lift and longer duration, while larger, 42mm intake and 37mm exhaust valves replace the stock 41/35mm sizes, and a pair of Mikuni 41mm Pro Series carburetors are substituted for the stock dual-throat Weber. The motor mods are capped off with a 2-into-1-into-2 exhaust system with aluminum mufflers, built for FBF by Muzzy R&D.

The result is an engine which Ferracci claims produces 88 horsepower, and which powered our test bike through the Carlsbad Raceway quarter-mile in 11.645 seconds at 118.26 mph, despite an overheated clutch. Compare this to the 12.44-second, 107.27-mph clocking for a stock 750 Sport, or the 12.06-second, 111.66-mph run recorded by our Pro Italia-modified project bike.

Turning his attention to the chassis, Ferracci ditches the stock 16-inch wheels in favor of a pair of 17-inch spun-aluminum hoops built by Mitchell for Performance Machine, in wide, 3.5-inch front and 4.5-inch rear sizes. These were shod with soft-compound Yokohama radial slicks on our test bike, but Ferracci says he plans to switch to Dunlop rubber in the future.

The front brakes are also upgraded, with twin Brembo 11-inch, floating, cast-iron discs grasped by PM four-piston calipers; a Grimeca master cylinder and steel-braided teflon lines offer improved lever feel.

The non-adjustable Marzocchi fork is left stock with the exception of a change to 10-weight oil in the factory-recommended volume, while a fully adjustable Fox shock replaces the stock Marzocchi unit at rear. Ferracci mounts the shock's remote reservoir under the seat, requiring the repositioning of some electrical components.

To find out just how race-ready a Daytona GP2 Replica really is, we entered ours in an ARRA club meeting at Willow Springs. But first, the bike had to be prepared to pass tech inspection. As the bike arrived from FBF, its only concession to racing's safety requirements was a crankcase breather catch bottle; none of the necessary nuts

Mikuni Pro Series 41mm flat-slide carburetors feed the potent V-Twin, which also features aftermarket rods, pistons and camshafts, and an FBF 2-into-2 exhaust system. Standard operating procedure for a racing Ducati includes ditching the cambelt covers, which makes for a purposeful appearance.

and bolts were as much as drilled to accept safety wire, so we had Pro Italia complete the remaining work.

Out at the racetrack, things got off to a slow start as much of Saturday's practice was spent tracing a loose fuel-pump connection and an intermittent ignition relay.

Sunday went much better. During the two brief practice sessions, I determined that while the engine performed magnificently, the bike suffered from a slight lack of ground clearance, dragging the mufflers on both sides and the brake pedal on the right, and that the stock fork springs felt too stiff, making the bike reluctant to hold its line under throttle.

When asked about these shortcomings, Ferracci said that the clearance problems on Cortez's bike were solved by fitting 2-inch-longer tubes between the exhaust collector and mufflers, and that the fork springs work fine once they're broken in.

I also felt the bike needed a steering damper badly, as it repeatedly shook its head cresting Willow's Turn Six. This trait would prove to be my undoing.

Race time came, and I got off to a fairly decent start. Fifth place became fourth when the leader pulled off with mechanical problems, and a pass put me into third position. "Bitchin'! A trophy will look great in the photos," I thought.

Wrong. Shortly thereafter, I hooked my outstretched knee on the inside edge of the track at Turn Six, wrenching my leg back, pulling off my knee puck, and setting up a godawful tankslapper that caused me to knock the bike out of gear. By the time I collected myself, I'd been repassed.

Braver men would have continued on undaunted—I settled for fourth.

Trophy or no trophy, the Fast By Ferracci Ducati 750 Sport Daytona GP2 Replica is impressive. Though the bike would benefit from additional race preparation—safety wire, steering damper and longer pipes—these things cost money. Ferracci informed us that the bike should really cost about $12,000 as is—and would be even more expensive with the aforementioned additions—except that Cagiva recoups some of its losses by selling the stock parts Ferracci removes.

But that needn't concern you. What should is that for just over 10 grand, you can buy a bike that is not just capable of winning a national championship: It already has.
—*Brian Catterson*

SHOOTOUT OF THE WORLD SUPERBIKE RIVALS

DUCATI 888 vs KAWASAKI ZX-7R

IN BENCH-RACING CIRCLES, A HOT topic for debate, as of late, is the issue of just what was the best bike/rider combination in Superbike racing last year?

Was it World Superbike Champion Raymond Roche riding his factory Ducati 888? Or could it have been U.S. Superbike Champion Doug Chandler on the Muzzy Kawasaki ZX-7?

A tough one to answer, especially considering that both men rode their machines to decisive victories in their respective series, while only meeting head-to-head on a couple of occasions. When Chandler dropped in on the World Superbike series, he scored a pair of wins in the process.

With the odds of setting up a Roche vs. Chandler title fight far from likely, we did the next best thing: booked a date in Las Vegas, Nevada, for a closed-circuit head butt of the 1991 production versions of both championship-winning machines. Both the Ducati 888 and the Kawasaki ZX-7R are limited-edition, higher-performance versions of more readily available sportbikes, the 888 based on the Ducati 851, and the ZX-7R sharing frame, most engine parts and some bodywork with the newly introduced Kawasaki ZX-7.

Las Vegas Motor Speedway, located a few miles north of town, was the venue for our Superbike showdown. The 1.6-mile, nine-turn road course offered a variety of turns ranging from high-speed sweepers to medium-speed U-turns to a slow, 90-degree bend. Some turns required hard, straight-line braking, while others called for trailing the brakes as the bikes were peeled in toward the corner's apex.

Race tuners will tell you that dynamometers don't lie, and riders claim the same can be said for lap times. However, the results of our lap times at Vegas can't be considered conclusive due to a minor difficulty with our ZX-7R test bike.

The ZX-R we picked up at Kawasaki prior to our track comparison had been flogged by another motorcycle publication, and was badly in need of fresh rubber. Kawasaki was kind enough to install a set of wheels from an unused ZX-7R, but these—despite the fact that they came directly from the factory—were not balanced. We soon discovered this oversight on the racetrack, where the bike pattered its front wheel to the extent that we couldn't get a good feeling for what was going on between the tire and the track, particularly under hard braking.

Despite the shuddering ride created by the unbalanced wheels, the ZX-R lapped the Vegas circuit at a pace only a half-second slower than the Ducati 888, leaving us wondering how much quicker it would have been with properly set-up wheels.

Although the day at the track didn't go as planned, it provided the opportunity to ride the two machines hard lap after lap, which usually exposes any weaknesses or subsequent deterioration in suspension or braking performance. The Ducati's Brembo stoppers did an exellent job of hauling the big red Twin down from high speed. However, the lever feel was on the soft side to begin

DUCATI 888 vs. KAWASAKI ZX-7R

Removal of the 7R's aluminum fuel tank allows unobstructed access to carburetor tops for jetting changes. Threaded boss on the frame spar is for mounting a steering damper, though one isn't included as standard equipment.

with, and pulled in even closer to the grip when subjected to repeated hard use. The ZX-7R, with Tokico calipers, delighted us with the best Kawasaki brakes we've experienced. The R stopped every bit as well as the 888, while maintaining a firm feel at the lever throughout our test. The rear brakes on both bikes performed well, not being overly sensitive nor causing unwanted wheel lockup, nor did they chatter as they approached lock-up.

Neither bike showed any sign of shock fade or suffered from too-soft fork springs, both problems common with many streetable sportbikes when put through their paces on a roadrace circuit. The 888 is equipped with an Öhlins remote-reservoir shock. Compression and rebound damping are easily adjusted by hand-turning accessible knobs. Spring pre-

load requires removal of the tail section for access with a spanner. Ride height can also be altered with an adjustable eccentric in the linkage rocker arm. Up front, an Öhlins inverted fork offers compression- and rebound-damping adjusters that can be altered with an allen wrench, and a threaded spring-preload adjuster is also provided.

The ZX-7R's Kayaba suspension components share the same assortment of adjustments (give or take a few clicks here and there). All of its damping adjusters, save for the shock's hand-turnable rebound knob, require a flat-blade screwdriver (or a dime) to turn their slotted screws. The upper shock mount is threaded to allow changes in ride height at the rear, while changing ride height in the front is easily accomplished, as there's unobstructed ac-

Fast-wearing sponge grips, spongy brake feel, a lagging tach, idiot lights that turned invisible in bright sunlight and a broken speedometer cable were bothersome, but did little to dampen our enthusiasm for the Ducati's wonderful engine and chassis.

Ventilated dry-clutch cover and an oil cooler below the front cylinder are items not found on the steet-legal Ducati 851, the basis for the 888. Other changes include larger cylinder bores, bigger valves, twin-nozzle fuel injectors and less restrictive exhaust pipes.

ZX-7R engine features pistons, cams, carburetors and transmission all focused on higher performance than the ZX-7's. For further gains, a race kit is also available.

cess to all pinch bolts holding the fork legs in place. Performing the same ride-height adjustment to the front of the 888 takes more time and patience.

With properly balanced wheels on the ZX-R, we continued with top-speed, dragstrip and street testing of our title contenders.

The Kawasaki took the nod in the top-speed department, registering 152 mph on the radar gun, topping the 888 by 5 mph. The Ducati was held back by its final gearing, which allowed the engine to run into the rev limiter in top gear, cheating the bike

of a few more mph. Both bikes showed very good straight-line stability at speeds of a buck fifty or so.

Both bikes slugged it out toe-to-toe when we ran them through the timing lights at Carlsbad Raceway. The 888 would leave the line with a lunge, the clutch fully engaged not far out of the hole, and grunt away, using the V-Twin's superior midrange torque. The ZX-R's tall first gear required a great deal of clutch slippage for some distance down the strip before the clutch could be fully engaged without bogging the engine. Even with such drastic differences in getting out of the gate, the green machine nipped the Italian stallion by a nose at the end of the 440-yard dash, turning a 10.82-second run at 129.68 mph to the 888's 10.84/128.20. Close enough, though, to call it a dead-heat.

Racetrack lapping and performance testing had failed to provide a clear winner, so we moved the bout outside the ropes and took the fight to the street.

Our initial riding impressions on public roads had us praising the 888 for its broad spread of power and its fuel injection's ridability, and cursing the ZX-R for its lack of low-end power and a first gear that's too tall for practical street duty. Pulling away from a stop on the ZX-R was a tedious task which soon grew old, especially around town. If the revs weren't held above 3500 rpm and the clutch wasn't slipped to the other side

of an intersection, the engine would stumble, bog and lurch—if it didn't stall outright.

Before writing this behavior off as the price to pay for riding a thorough-bred racer, we richened the air/fuel mixure by raising the carburetor needles .040 inch. As with other EPA-approved bikes, the needles don't have multiple clip-groves, so small-diameter washers were slipped on the

The R-model's 41mm Kayaba upside-down fork offers more adjustability than the standard ZX-7 fork and weighs less.

Fuel-injection brain and the Öhlins shock's remote reservoir reside in the Ducati's tailsection. Swingarm-mounted fender is made of lightweight carbon-fiber.

DUCATI 888
vs.
KAWASAKI ZX-7R

needle under the clip, thus raising the needle, and allowing increased fuel flow through the needle jet.

Unbelievable. Improvement of the ZX-R's street manners was so dramatic that it called for a re-think of our verdict—which, to that point, had been to sentence the ZX-7R to life without parole on the racetrack. A smooth rollaway could now be accomplished, the tall first gear was no longer a problem and there wasn't a hint of the previous "buck 'n' surge" routine. Still, there's one thing to bear in mind while riding the ZX-R: Its flat-slide carburetors are not as forgiving of ham-fisted operation as are CV carbs, or as is the 888's Weber-Marelli fuel injection, which yields crisp response if whacked open at any rpm. At engine speeds below 5500 rpm, the ZX-R's throttle must be rolled on smoothly for best results. Once above the 6000-rpm mark, snapping the throttle wide-open results in immediate engine response and a rush of acceleration, followed by another surge when the Four comes on the cam at 9000 rpm. From there, it pulls very strongly to the 12,500-rpm redline. Shifting is smooth, quiet and requires light effort at the lever—the ZX-7R is easily the slickest-shifting Kawasaki in recent memory.

The 888 plugs away from a stop without hassle, quickens its pace at 4000 rpm and outraces the tachometer, reaching the 10,000-rpm rev limiter while the tach needle indicates just 9400 rpm. Short-shifting is the key to uninterrupted power delivery from the 888's mill while in the lower three gears. The Duck has a light throttle-return spring, which is easy on the wrist but which allows unintentional rider-induced throttle fluctuation on bumpy roads and freeway joints, causing minor engine surge.

While the ZX-7R shifts slickly, the 888's gearbox action is better still—very light and precise. However, finding neutral is next to impossible with the engine running, and once you have found it, the neutral light doesn't illuminate brightly enough for daylight viewing.

As you can see, each of these bikes has a full complement of finely honed skills that will keep lesser machines pinned agianst the ropes, and each has an impressive knockout punch. So, just how do we judge this clash of the Superbike surrogates? Well, based on performance, it would be easy to call the match a draw. But take a look at things like price, warranty and street-legality. And here, given that the ZX-7R is nearly $12,000 cheaper, that it comes with a warranty (while the Ducati has none) and is 50-state legal (while the 888 is a track-use only proposition), the decision is unanimous: We'll take the Kawasaki.

SPECIFICATIONS	Ducati 888	Kawasaki ZX-7R
GENERAL		
List price	$20,400	$8999
Warranty	none	12 mo./unlimited mi.
ENGINE & DRIVETRAIN		
Engine	liquid-cooled, four-stroke V-Twin	liquid-cooled, four-stroke inline-Four
Bore x stroke	94.0 x 64.0mm	71.0 x 47.3mm
Displacement	888cc	749cc
Compression ratio	11.0:1	11.5:1
Valve train	dohc, four valves per cylinder, desmodromic acutation, shim adjustment	dohc, four valves per cylinder, shim adjustment
Valve adj. intervals	1860 mi.	6,000 mi.
Carburetion	fuel injection	(4) 39mm Keihin
Electrical power	350w	430w
CHASSIS		
Weight:		
Tank empty	469 lb.	460 lb.
Tank full	501 lb.	489 lb.
Fuel capacity	5.3 gal.	4.8 gal.
Wheelbase	55.5 in.	55.5 in
Rake/trail	24.0°/3.7 in.	24.5°/3.7 in.
Seat height	30.5 in.	30.3 in.
GVWR	na	728 lb.
Load capacity (tank full)	na	239 lb.
SUSPENSION & TIRES		
Front suspension:		
Claimed wheel travel	4.7 in.	4.7 in.
Adjustments	compression and rebound damping, spring preload	compression and rebound damping, spring preload
Rear suspension:		
Claimed wheel travel	4.3 in.	5.3 in.
Adjustments	compression and rebound damping, spring preload	compression and rebound damping, spring preload
Tires:		
Front	120/70 ZR17 Dunlop Sportmax Radial	120/70 VR17 Michelin Hi-Sport Radial
Rear	180/50 VR17 Dunlop Sportmax Radial	180/55 VR17 Michelin Hi-Sport Radial
PERFORMANCE		
¼ mi.	10.84 sec. @ 128.20 mph	10.82 sec. @ 129.68 mph
0-60 mph	3.1 sec.	3.7 sec.
Top gear time to speed, sec.		
40-60 mph	4.2	3.7
60-80 mph	3.5	4.3
Measured top speed	147 mph	152 mph
Engine speed at 60 mph	3990 rpm	4630 rpm
FUEL MILEAGE		
High/low/avg.	50/37/43 mpg	34/24/30 mpg
Avg. range inc. reserve	228 mi.	144 mi.
BRAKING DISTANCE		
from 30 mph	22 ft.	23 ft.
from 60 mph	102 ft.	103 ft.

CYCLE WORLD ON BMW 1964-1973
CYCLE WORLD ON BMW 1974-1980
CYCLE WORLD ON DUCATI 1962-1980
CYCLE WORLD ON HARLEY-DAVIDSON 1968-1978
CYCLE WORLD ON HARLEY-DAVIDSON 1978-1983
CYCLE WORLD ON HARLEY-DAVIDSON 1983-1987
CYCLE WORLD ON HARLEY-DAVIDSON 1987-1990
CYCLE WORLD ON HONDA 1968-1971
CYCLE WORLD ON HUSQVANA 1966-1976
CYCLE WORLD ON HUSQVANA 1977-1984
CYCLE WORLD ON KAWASAKI 1966-1971
CYCLE WORLD ON KAWASAKI OFF-ROAD BIKES 1972-1976
CYCLE WORLD ON TRIUMPH 1962-1967
CYCLE WORLD ON TRIUMPH 1972-1987
CYCLE WORLD ON SUZUKI 1967-1970
CYCLE WORLD ON SUZUKI OFF-ROAD BIKES 1971-1976
CYCLE WORLD ON YAMAHA 1962-1969
CYCLE WORLD ON YAMAHA OFF-ROAD BIKES 1970-1974

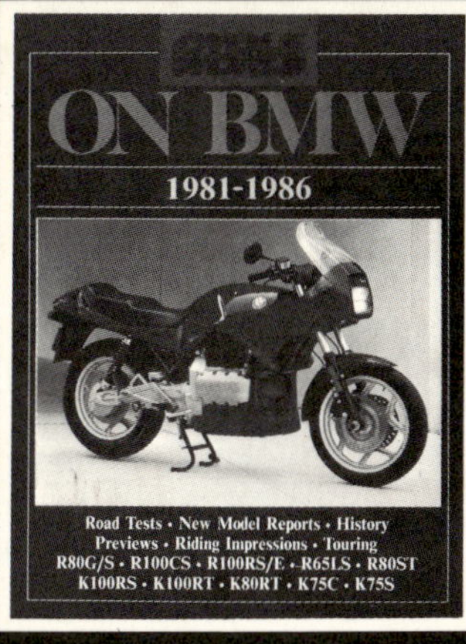

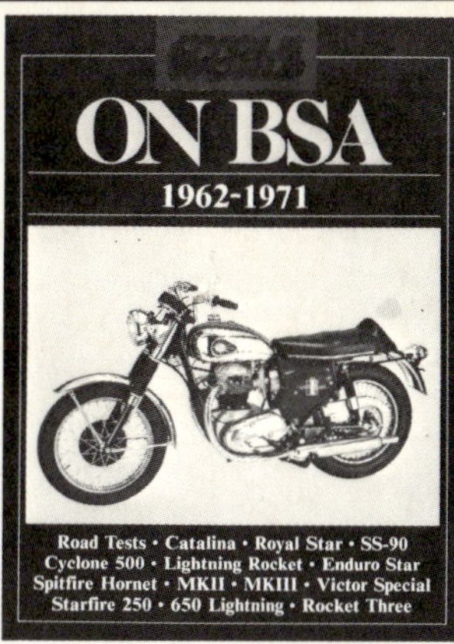

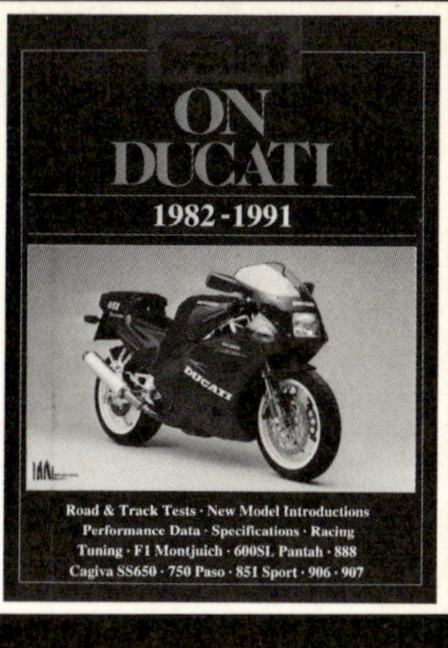

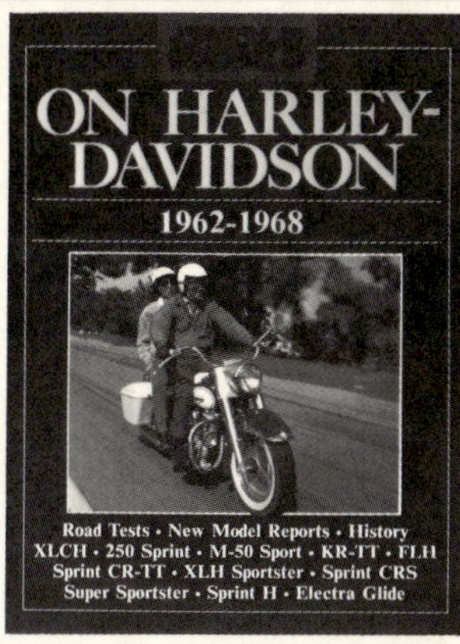

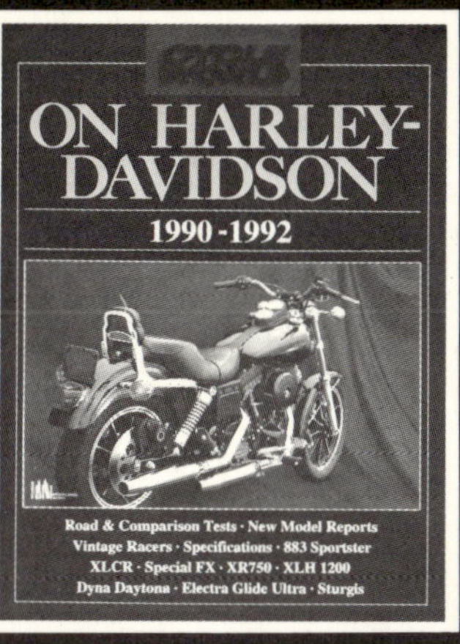

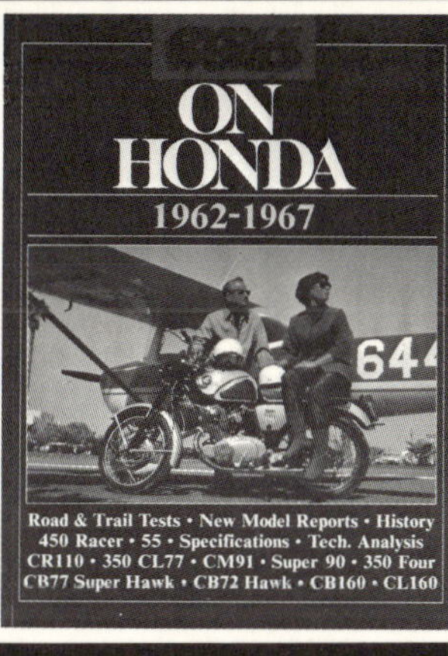

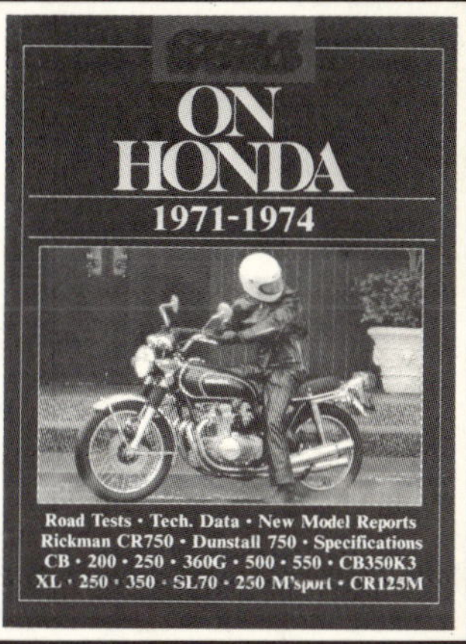

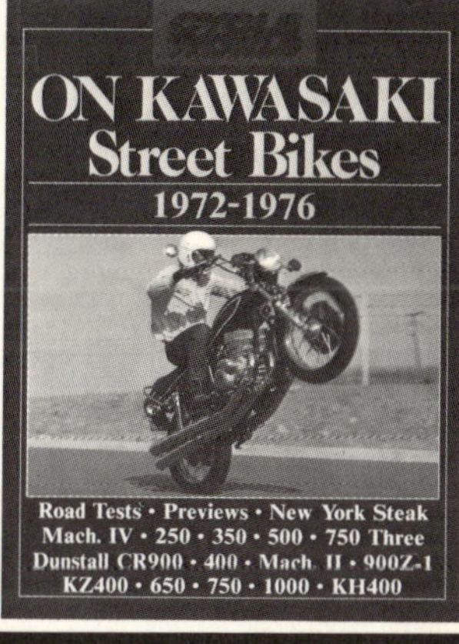

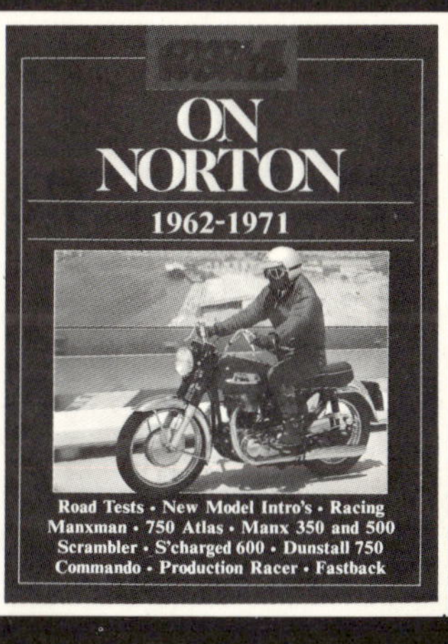

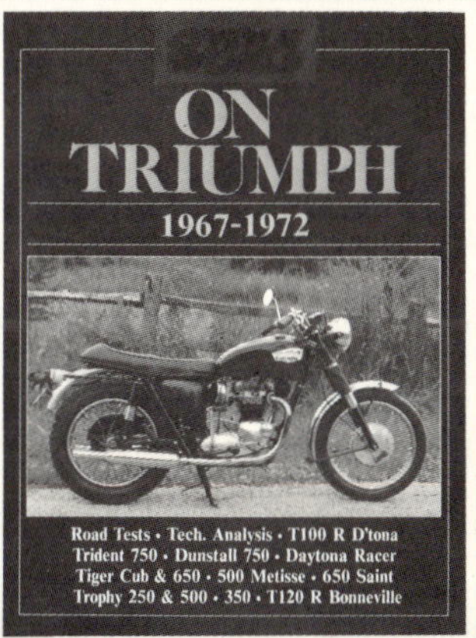

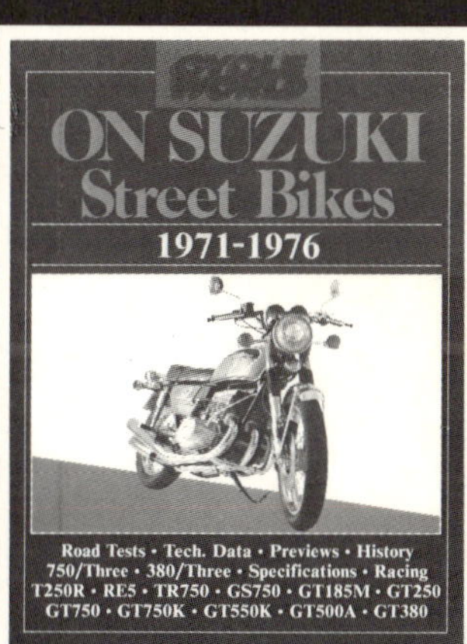

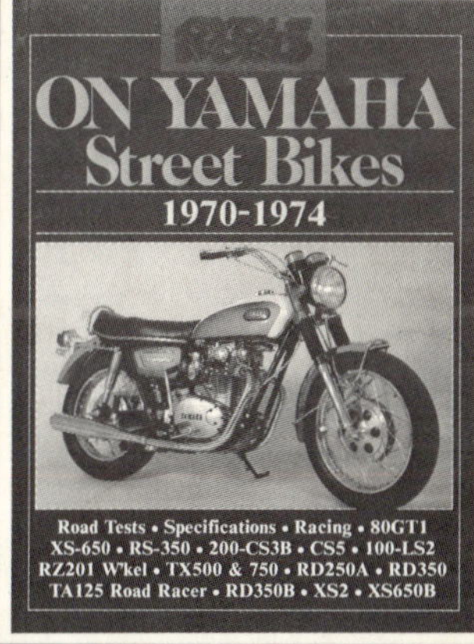

DISTRIBUTED BY

CarTech,
11481 Kost Dam Road,
North Branch,
MN 55056, USA
Phone: 800 551 4754 & 612 583 3471
Fax: 612 583 2023

Brooklands Books Ltd,
PO Box 146,
Cobham, Surrey KT11 1LG
England
Phone: 0932 865051
Fax: 0932 868803

ISBN 1 85520 2069

SUZUKI SJ

Gold Portfolio

1971-1997

**Road & Comparison Tests • Model Introductions
Performance & Technical Data • Buying Used
Janspeed • Allard • Pick-up • Brute • LJ80 & 81
Samurai • Santana • Sierra • 410 • 413 • LWB**

ABOUT BROOKLANDS BOOKS

As a company Brooklands Books are dedicated to preserving motoring and motorcycling literature for enthusiasts. They have in print over 700 titles which deal with various aspects of motoring. A guide to each series is given below.

REGULAR BROOKLANDS BOOKS. Collected road tests, model descriptions, driving impressions and other articles on individual models and marques - plus muscle car compilations - taken from a wide variety of car magazines in Britain, North America and Australia. Filled with informed and reliable comment, specifications, performance data, buying used reports and other details, these books provide a fine opportunity to absorb all relevant information on the car you own, are thinking of buying or restoring, or perhaps simply admire.

BROOKLANDS 'COLLECTIONS'. Similar to 'Regular' Brooklands books, but lower priced and fewer pages.

GOLD PORTFOLIO SERIES. Again drawing on material from a wide range of motoring and motorcycling magazines, books in this series are devoted to desirable cars, bikes and three-wheelers from Britain, the Continent and North America. They have almost twice as many pages and illustrations as 'Regular' Brooklands Books and are an unparalleled source of interest and knowledge on the world's most sought-after vehicles

MUSCLE, PERFORMANCE & MILITARY PORTFOLIOS. The titles in these categories deal respectively with US and British muscle cars, performance marques and military subjects and have half as many articles again as the 'Regular' Brooklands Books.

LIMITED EDITIONS The contents of these books are similar to our Regular Brooklands Books and Gold Portfolios. However due to the specialised subject matter print runs will rarely be greater than 500 copies.

BROOKLANDS RACING SERIES. These books are similar in size and quality to our Gold Portfolio series. They contain contemporary race reports taken in the main from British and American journals. They currently cover the great Le Mans and Mille Miglia races and it is our intention to expand the series further.

PRACTICAL CLASSICS SERIES. Comprehensive restorers' guides, compiled from the pages of 'Practical Classics' magazine and based on 'hands-on' experience. All restoration tasks are covered.

ROAD & TRACK SERIES. Collected tests, comparisons, new model introductions, racing and touring articles and other material from the internationally popular American magazine 'Road & Track'.

CAR and DRIVER SERIES. Similar collections from 'Car and Driver' magazine, USA. Once again, these books supply a wealth of information on numerous models, in a package easy both to read and to keep.

CYCLE WORLD SERIES. Compiled exclusively from the US magazine 'Cycle World'. Included: on and off-road tests, technical information, touring and racing articles, comparisons and other material on a wide range of bikes.

HOT ROD 'ON GREAT AMERICAN ENGINES' SERIES. Musclecar and high performance material drawn from Hot Rod, Car Craft and other Petersen publications on how to maintain, tune, repair, restore and modify the popular power plants of the musclecar era.

FACTORY MANUALS. These are original unedited factory publications reissued under license. They include workshop manuals, parts manuals and owners manuals/handbooks. Far more detailed than the 'condensed' literature widely available, they are essential possessions for owners and restorers and are highly recommended. We also include some official sales brochures within this series.

WORKSHOP MANUALS - OWNERS EDITIONS. This fast growing series, written and illustrated by experts, cover servicing, overhaul and repair for DIY owners and restorers. These are mainly large format books containing over 200 illustrations and some contain advice on buying a used model. Some are available as 'glove-box' editions.

BROOKLANDS GENERAL RESTORATION & TECHNICAL BOOKS. Practical guides for owners wishing to restore or upgrade their cars. Some of these titles are drawn from the pages of 'Hot Rod' magazine and fall into our 'Restoration Tips & Techniques' or 'Performance Tuning' categories. All contain detailed and expert text, together with hundreds of explanatory photos.

BROOKLANDS REISSUES OF MAGAZINES. Early copies of 'Road & Track', 'Hot Rod' and 'Autosport'. Economically priced, these reissues are a boon to collectors.

Send for catalogue and full list to:

Brooklands Books Ltd., PO Box 146, Cobham, Surrey KT11 1LG, England Phone: 01932 865051 Fax: 01932 868803
Brooklands Books Ltd, 1/81 Darley St., PO Box 199, Mona Vale, NSW 2103, Australia Phone: 2 9997 8428 Fax: 2 9979 5799
CarTech, 11481 Kost Dam Road, North Branch, MN 55056, USA Phone 800 551 4754 & 612 583 3471 Fax: 612 583 2023
Motorbooks International, Osceola, Wisconsin 54020, USA Phone 715 294 3345 & 800 826 6600 Fax: 715 294 4448